THOMAS EARP
Eminent Victorian Sculptor

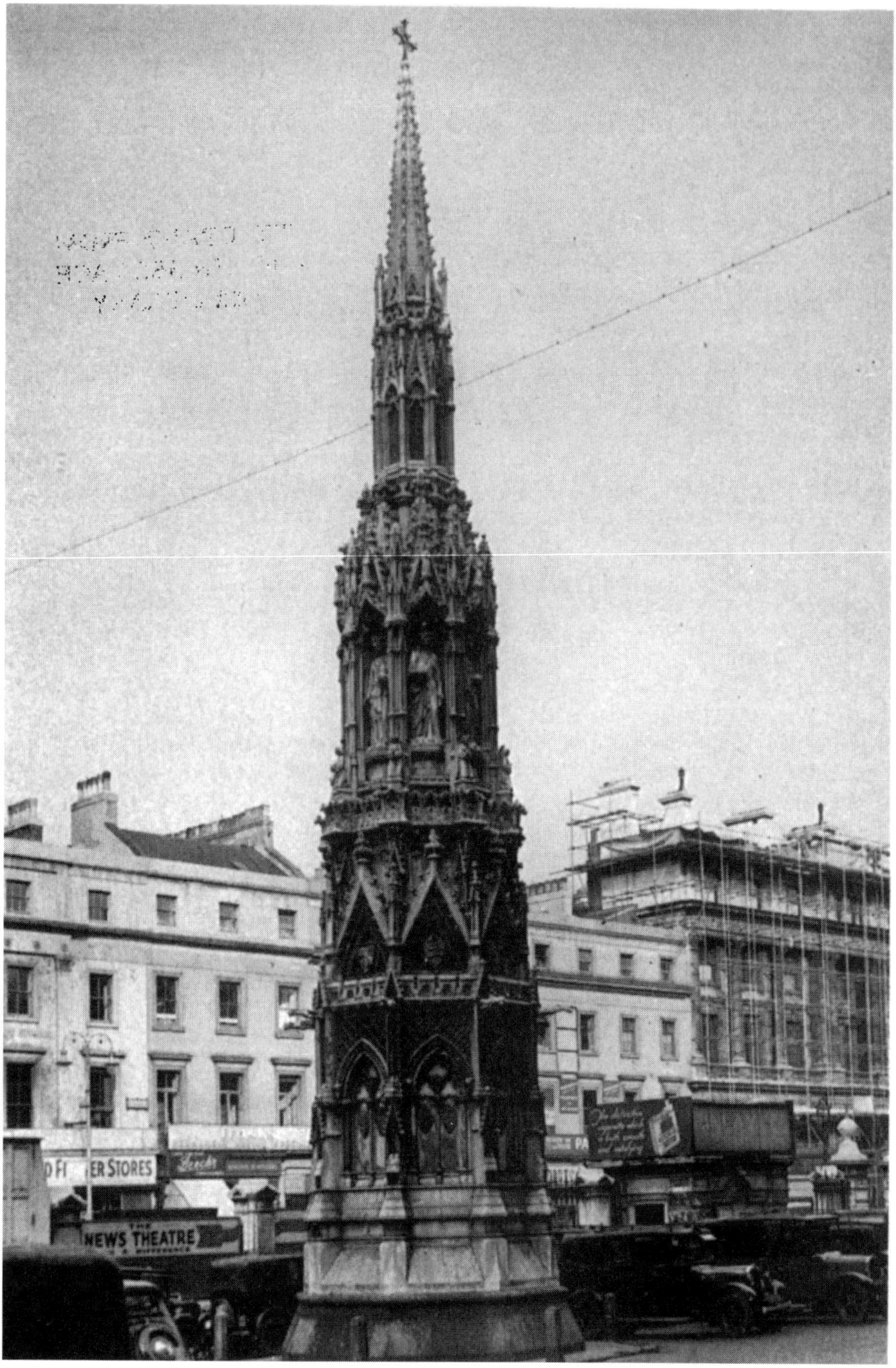

Eleanor Cross, 1863. The monument stands outside Charing Cross Station, London. (NMR)

THOMAS EARP
Eminent Victorian Sculptor

by

Anthony Mitchell and Olive Mitchell

BARON
BUCKINGHAM
MMII

PUBLISHED BY BARRACUDA BOOKS IN 1990
AND IN THIS SECOND EDITION BY
BARON BOOKS OF BUCKINGHAM IN 2002
AND PRODUCED BY BOOKCRAFT

ISBN 0 86023 669 2

Contents

ACKNOWLEDGEMENTS

Our thanks are due to the staffs of innumerable public libraries for the kind assistance and interest shown to us in the course of our investigations; also to the librarians of the Royal Institute of British Architects, the Council for the Care of Churches, the Lambeth Palace Library, the Minet Library of Camberwell, the Guildhall Library and Record Office, London, the Greater London Record Office, the Nottinghamshire and Derbyshire County Record Offices, the Nottinghamshire Family History Society, and the staffs of the British Library and of the Public Record Office; the helpful staff in the Architectural Section of the Royal Commission on Historical Monuments of England and Wales, and for the help of many history societies, not to mention the countless clergy, incumbents and caretakers who have always gone to great trouble to allow us access to many of the pieces of work described in this book. We also thank Mr David Neil-Smith for supplying pictures of St Saviour's, South Hampstead, Canon Povey for the picture from All Saints, Clifton, Bedfordshire, and Reverend Geoffrey Hurst for the picture from St Marie's Cathedral, Sheffield. Finally, the Drawing Room of Arundel Castle is reproduced by kind permission of His Grace the Duke of Norfolk, who has also kindly contributed a Foreword to this edition.

DEDICATION

To our family for their encouragement and interest.

Foreword by his Grace the Duke of Norfolk

I am pleased to contribute a foreword for this new extended second edition of Anthony Mitchell's book about his own grandfather, Thomas Earp, the eminent Victorian sculptor, written in collaboration with his wife Olive Mitchell.

I personally am privileged to possess an example of work by Thomas Earp, in the form of our chimneypiece in the Drawing Room of Arundel Castle.

Norfolk.

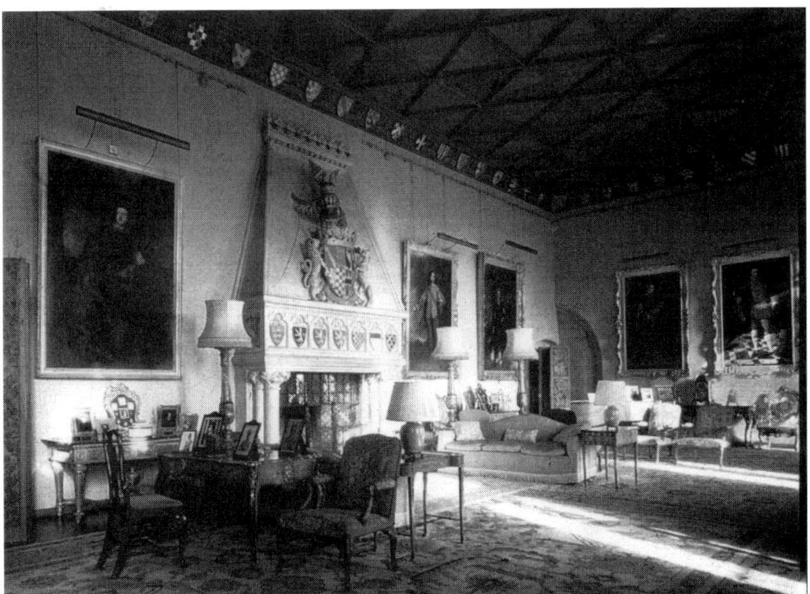

The drawing-room, Arundel Castle, showing Earp's chimney-piece. (N)

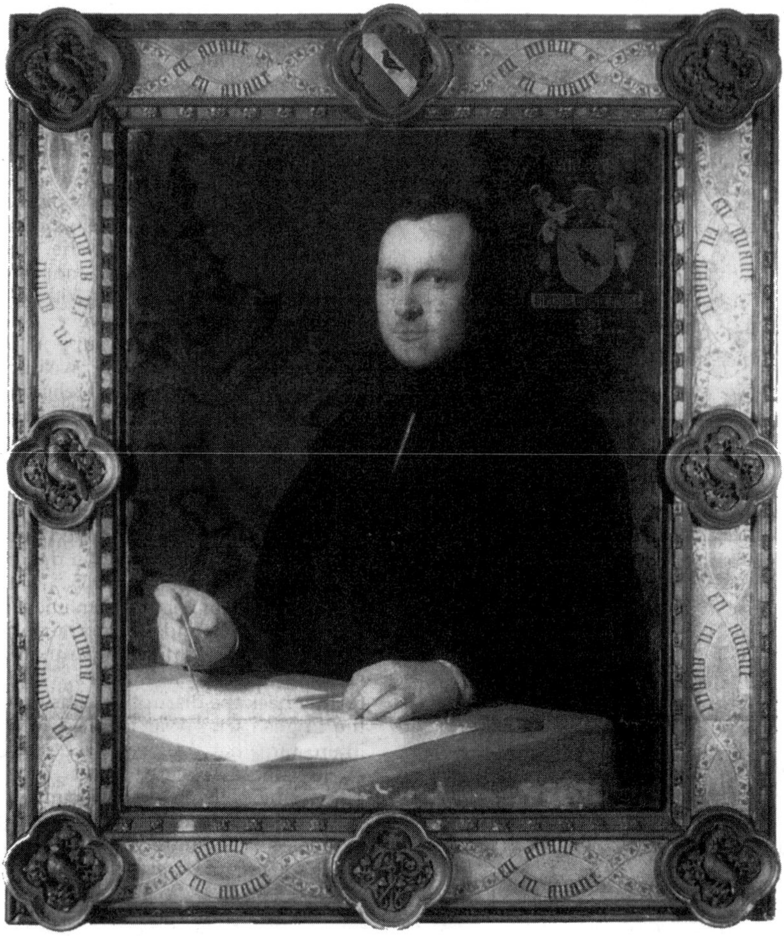

Augustus Welby Pugin.

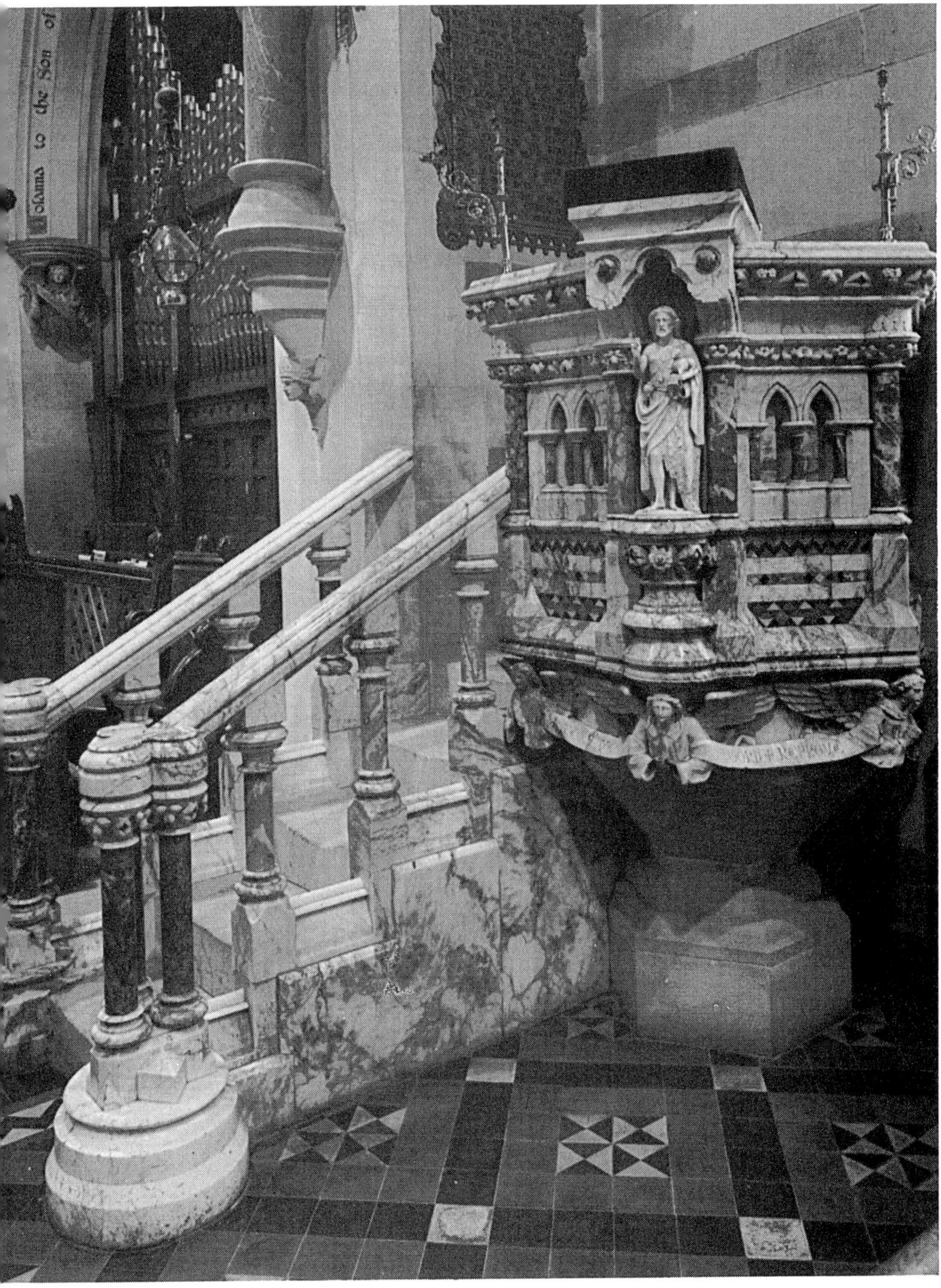

St John the Baptist, Huntley: pulpit. (NMR)

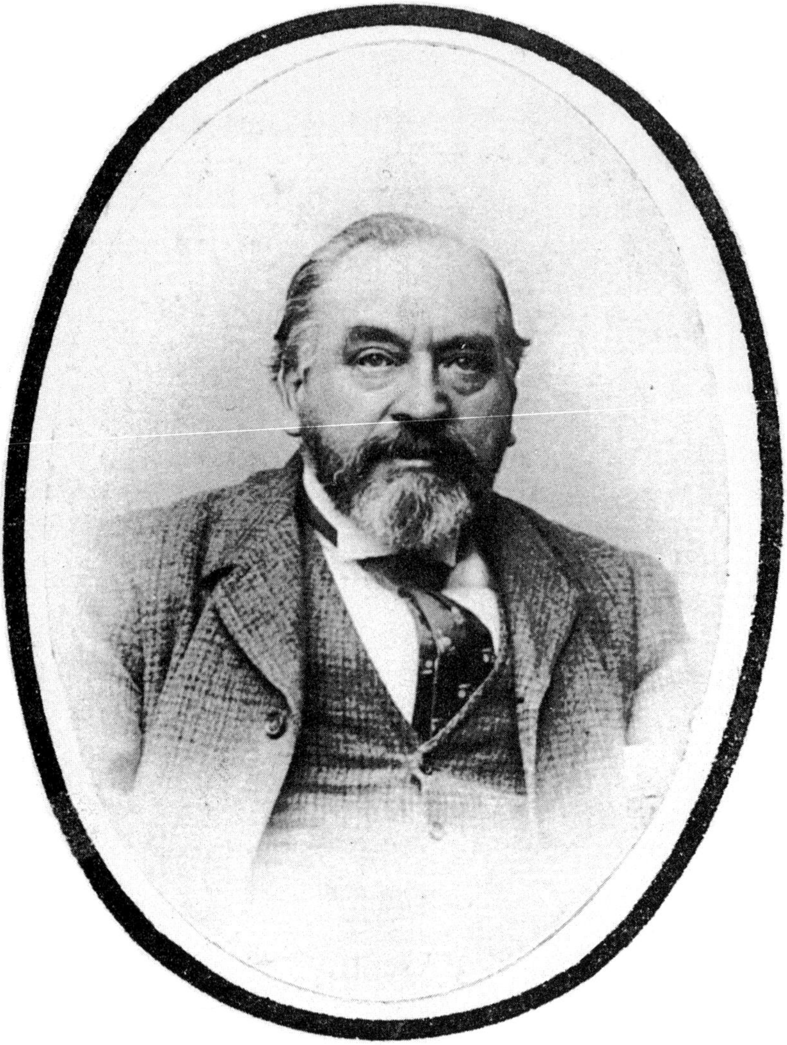

Thomas Earp (1828-1893).

Workfolk of Nottingham

Thomas Earp was born in 1828 in Nottingham to Thomas and Margaret Earp, and baptised in the great church of St Mary in April of that year. After him came a brother, Henry, and four sisters, Ann, Emma, Matilda and Eliza, and lastly another brother, Alexander Joseph.

The times during which young Thomas spent his childhood were turbulent ones. Before he was ten years old three monarchs had occupied the British throne. Society was undergoing the turmoil of the Industrial Revolution and Nottingham was expanding through economic growth in the Vale of Trent. Canals had improved communication with the rest of the country and in 1839 the railway came. Nottingham had long been noted for the making of lace and the framework knitting industry had begun to grow, though remaining family-based. Bobbinet began to be produced in large quantities due to the invention of the bobbinet machine by John Heathcoat. There was a resultant increase in Nottingham's population as people were drawn in from the surrounding countryside and it seems that Thomas Earp senior, who was born in King's Newton in neighbouring Derbyshire, was attracted by the growing opportunities and made his home in Nottingham with Margaret Jackson from Belper.

Nottingham's chief industry was suffering alternating periods of prosperity and recession throughout the early 1800s. When young Thomas was born his father was a lace-maker; later he lived and ran a business as a commission-agent for bobbinet in Derby Street, north-west of the city. He then moved to Bromley Place, a turning off Angel Row that faces the old market place. Eventually he went to live in Norton's Place, Castle Terrace, not far from Nottingham Castle itself. It is probable that, as lace-making became more mechanised, the hand craft declined and Thomas's father found it more opportune to practise as a commission agent. Subsequently he earned his living as an agent for the sale of starch, a commodity much in demand for use in the linen industry, another of Nottingham's specialities.

The lacemakers lived in tall apartments, the top floors of which had long windows extending their whole length, to provide the maximum light for work. Pastimes consisted chiefly of pugilism and race meetings, but an evangelical revival took place about the 1840s. One John Wright established a subscription library, and William Felkin, later Mayor of Nottingham, exercised great influence in the interests of the community. The year 1830 saw the last public whipping, and 1831 the last public execution.

There was great depression in the lace trade in 1837, and relief committees were set up. Trade improved in 1843, only to be followed by another recession in 1847. When trade improved again a branch of the National Charter Association was formed, but antipathy developed between Chartist and 'middle class' shopkeepers. The Lacemakers' Society appeared in the 1850s.

We have no absolute knowledge of where young Thomas Earp went to school, but it was probably the Nottingham Free School, where he was most likely soundly beaten by the headmaster, Reverend Doctor Wood, or by his assistant, Reverend Samuel Lund. Under this stern spiritual tutelage, for which the headmaster and his assistant were both reprimanded in due course by the School Committee, Thomas benefitted as intended by the school regulations, by which each scholar was taught grammar in one of six classes, into which they were divided by the head, who personally directed the tuition and the books used, and held half-yearly examinations. The school holidays consisted of two days at Easter, two days at Whitsun, two days off for the annual Goose Fair, and one day for Good Friday. Every Saturday afternoon was a half-holiday, and there was one hour less on Wednesday afternoon. There was one month's holiday each at Christmas and in midsummer. A master's salary was £70 a year. We have it on record that a writing master, Mr Hemm, put in for a rise in salary after sixteen years' service. In the following year his resignation was reported in the Borough Records.

When school ended for Thomas, thought had to be given to earning his living. The family did not enjoy a substantial income and his father did not derive much profit from being an agent for bobbinet. Much of his earnings were derived from work as a handyman or craftsman at a variety of trades, particularly a carpenter's joiner for firms of builders. Young Thomas showed great interest and aptitude for all forms of these crafts and his father felt he should be allowed to develop these skills.

In many of Britain's major cities the Government was setting up schools of Art and Design, and one such was opened in Nottingham on 1 April 1843 with 110 students, all 'of good character'. Thomas was among them. Its ostensible purpose was the 'Elementary Instructions, Instruction in Design for Manufacture and in the Historic Principles and Practice of Ornamental Arts'. Early subscribers to the school were leading lace-manufacturers in the city. The fees for boys were 4s per month, and for girls 2s. The bulk of the students were from the local lace industry. It was doubtless intended that the school would serve the needs of the lace industry. However, conflict soon developed between the broader concepts of fine arts and the needs of the industry. As an indication of how things went, by 1845 the principal was James Hammersley, a landscape painter.

In spite of this being one of the worst periods for the lace trade, enough money was available for Thomas to undergo some training. He regularly attended the School of Art and Design. On the route home he would often pause and watch work on the site of a new church in Derby Street being built for the Roman Catholics. By talking to workmen, he learnt the contractor was George Myers, and that Myers owned an extensive works on the South Bank of the Thames in London.

The prospect of entering the building profession and using his talents in some of its ancillary crafts attracted young Thomas, and he took to working with the builders and craftsmen in his spare time after school. When his studies were completed he took up full-time work on the Derby Street site.

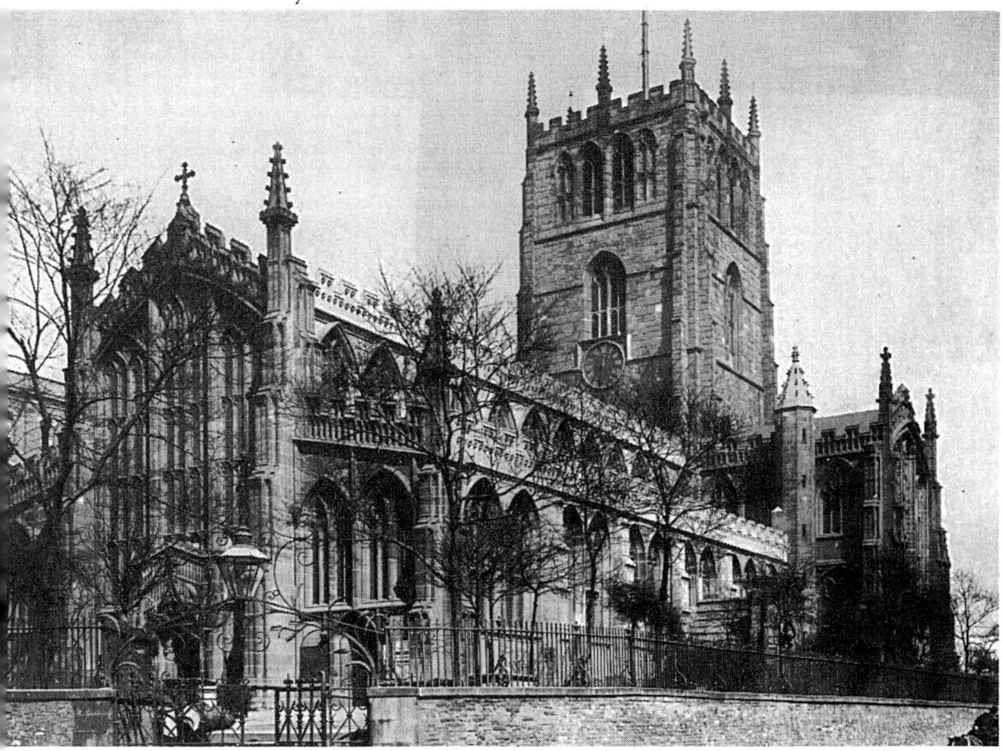

Church of St Mary, Nottingham — where Thomas Earp was baptised. (NMR)

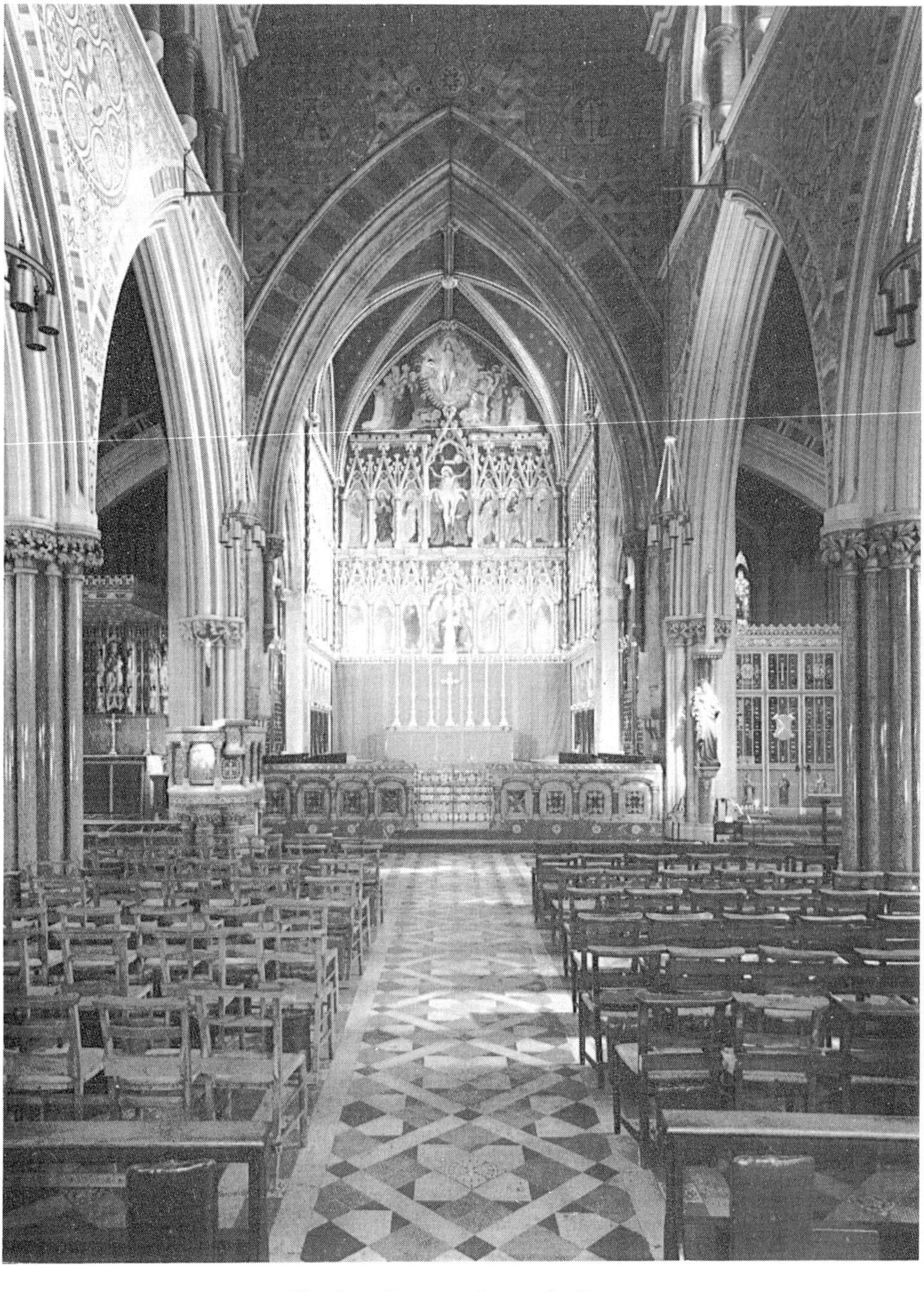

All Saints, Margaret Street: the Nave.

The Lambeth Craftsmen

Thomas Earp's career began under the tutelage of George Myers and Augustus Welby Pugin, partners in the upsurge of building that followed the fire that destroyed the old Houses of Parliament in 1834.

In London, entire schools of modelling, stone- and wood-carving sprang into being around the site of the Westminster re-building, and the demand for workers and craftsmen spread throughout the entire country. Charles Eastlake, in *The History of the Gothic Revival* observed: 'It would be impossible to over-rate the influence brought to bear on decorative sculpture by the encouragement given to those arts during the progress of the work at Westminster'.

Sir Charles Barry and Augustus Welby Northmore Pugin were co-architects in the reconstruction of the Houses of Parliament. It was the latter with whom the style known as 'Victorian Gothic' is mainly associated. To Pugin Gothic architecture was a complete way of life. In his book *True Principles of Pointed or Christian Architecture* he defended Gothic Architecture on various grounds, not least for practical reasons such as that a steep roof was better for a wet climate. He also argued that it was the only true style for a Christian church symbolising 'upwardness' in contrast to Classicism, which he considered symbolised 'worldliness'.

By making a special study of the details of Gothic Architecture Pugin encouraged others to do the same. Incongruously, however, this doyen of all ecclesiastical architects began his working life designing stage sets for ballets at Drury Lane.

It horrified his father, the elder Pugin, who had fled from France during the French Revolution some 30 or 40 years previously. On his arrival in England he had found work at the office of John Nash, the designer of the Royal Pavilion at Brighton, and had hoped his son would follow in his father's footsteps but, to make matters worse, the young Pugin instead turned his mind to the designing of ships, and, to risk creating a pun, 'floated' a business which did not prove profitable. To perpetrate another pun, the enterprise 'sank' and young Pugin landed in a debtor's prison.

When he came out financial prospects improved and he started at long last with the building trade, designing and building his own house in Salisbury.

He became a convert to the Catholic faith in 1834. Three years later he became professor of architecture at Oscott College and began his prodigious output of writings proclaiming his principles concerning church architecture.

He also embarked fully on his career of designing churches. One of the earliest of these was the Catholic Church of St Mary, Derby, of which the builders were a partnership of Richard Wilson and George Myers.

The result was so satisfactory that Pugin declared George Myers to be 'the very man I want'.

George Myers was described by Sir Gilbert Scott as 'a strange rough man from Hull'. Whatever may be inferred from this statement there is no doubt that Myers became one of the leading builders of the 19th century, playing a leading role in the country's building boom. In addition to fulfilling commissions for Pugin, Myers worked for other architects, including William Butterfield, whose church in London's Margaret Street was completed about the year 1850.

Myers also built hospitals, public buildings, railway stations, docks and prisons throughout the whole of his immense career. He had even built his own railway line, a branch from the London and Southampton main line to feed extensive building works at Aldershot to house troops training for the Crimean war.

Myers' workshops stood in Belvedere Road, Lambeth, and backed on to the River Thames where barges were constantly delivering and taking aboard merchandise. This place was known as Ordnance Wharf and Myers shared it with William Gladdish and Thomas Nunn, cement merchants and lime burners, on one side, while on the other was the wharf belonging to the Cheesewing Granite Company, known as 'Cement Wharf'.

Accordingly Thomas Earp in 1849 took leave of his parents, his brothers Henry and Alexander, and of his sisters, and left Nottingham to journey south. He joined Myers' teams of apprentices at Ordnance Wharf and quickly earned the reputation of being one of Myers' 'most skilful assistants'. It cannot be denied that it was under Myers, and indirectly under Pugin also, that Thomas Earp developed the skills which prompted many later chroniclers of the Victorian scene to call Earp 'the doyen of Victorian sculptors'.

Thomas Earp found his lodging at Addington Place, which may have been the present-day Addington Street, which is on the corner of York Road near the Lying-in Hospital. It was within easy walking distance of Ordnance Wharf. It was here that he met and courted Isabella Low, the daughter of a naval officer, and married her in the year following his arrival in London.

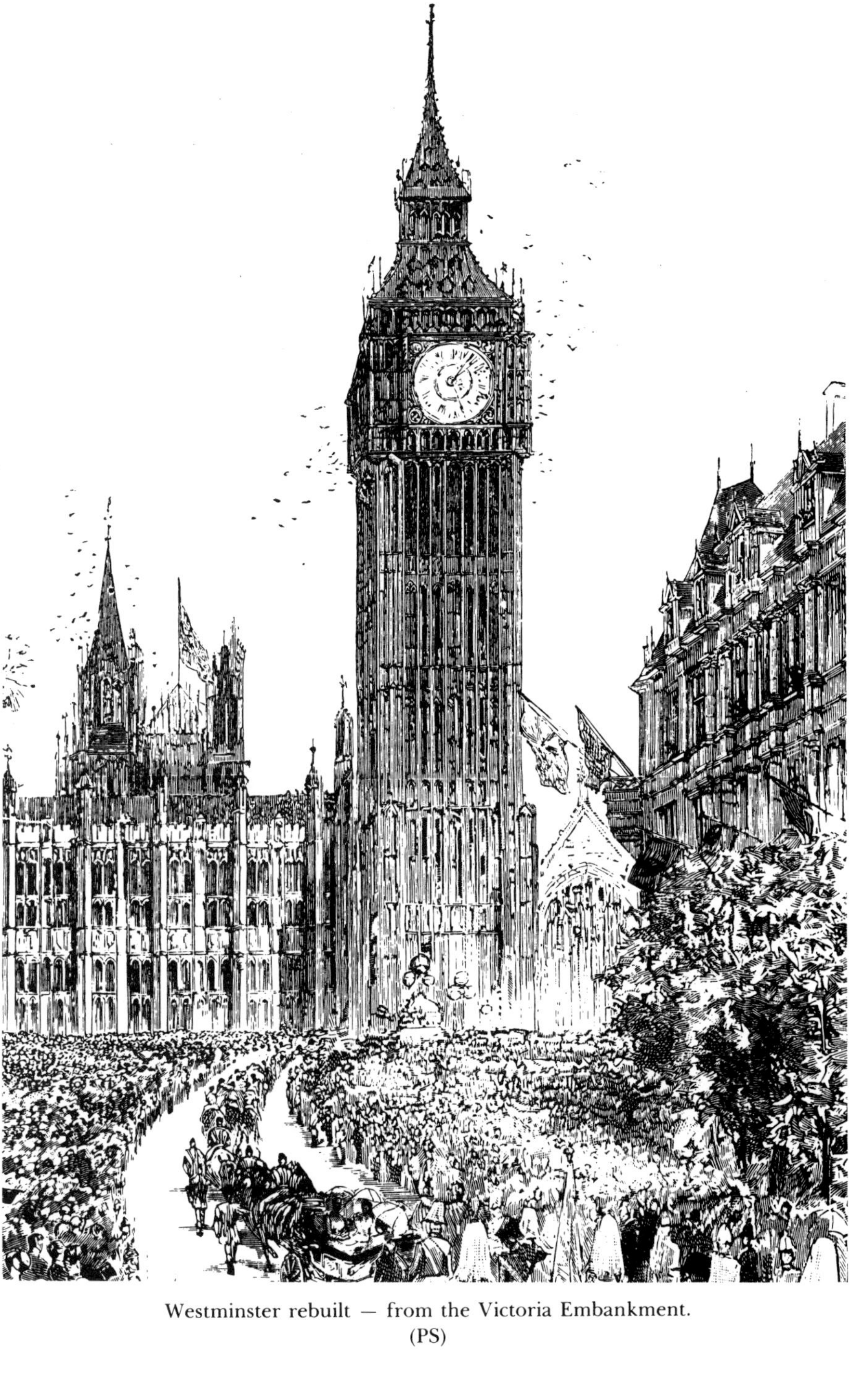

Westminster rebuilt — from the Victoria Embankment.
(PS)

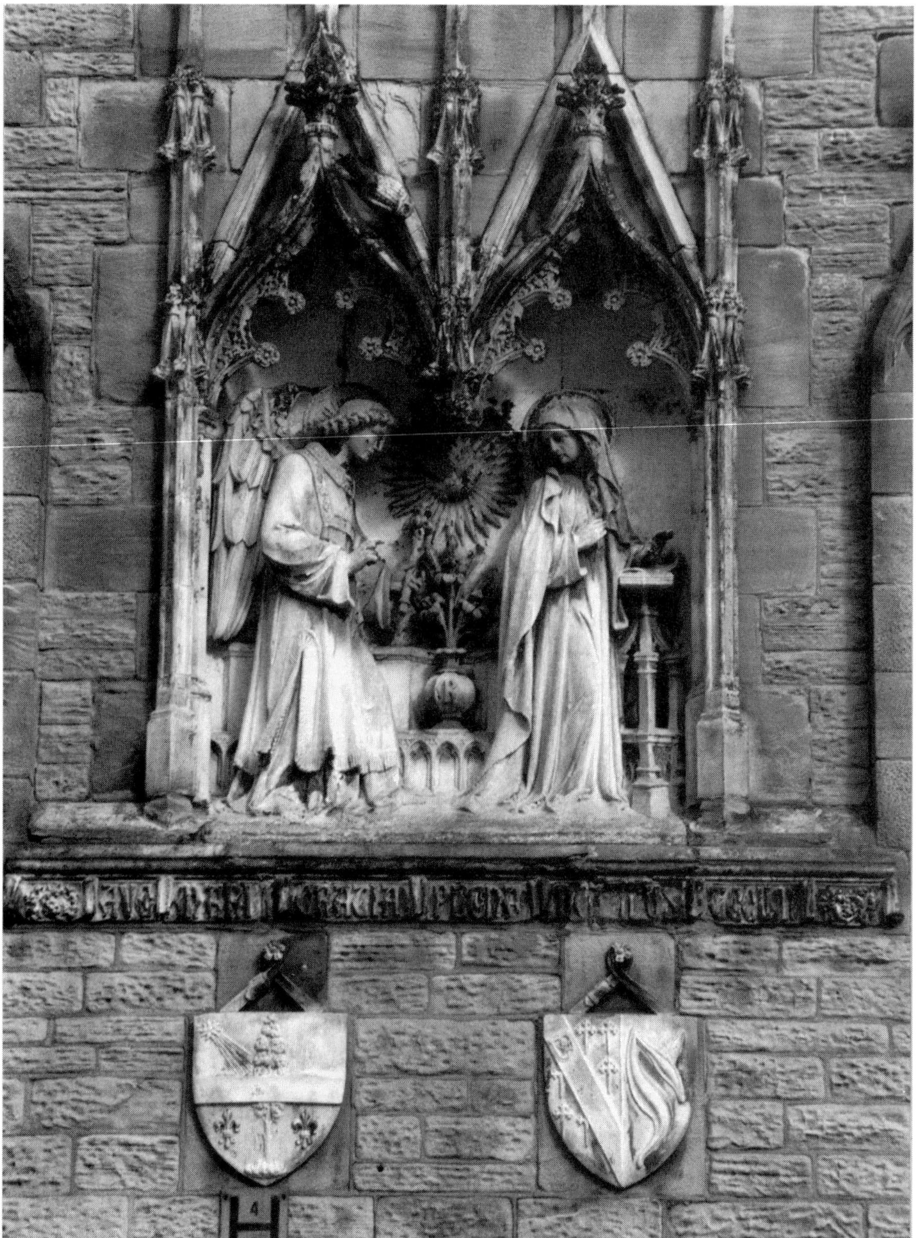

St Marie's Church (now Cathedral), Sheffield: Annunciation sculpture on outer wall. (GH)

Models of Excellence

It was not long after Thomas started work in South London that he was given his first important assignment within the firm of George Myers. This was at the new Catholic Church in Sheffield, called St Marie.

Dedicated to the Blessed Virgin Mary, it was named in the French style 'Saint-Marie' because of the influence of Pugin through his French extraction: he was responsible for much of the interior decoration and inspired the designs of the architects, Matthew Hadfield and John Grey Weightman. The church came about through the desires of the founder, a Father Pratt, who was an energetic protagonist in the cause of re-establishing the Roman Catholic Church in England. Charles Eastlake considered the building a 'model of excellence'. Pugin designed the reredos, the high altar and the font, and Myers was commissioned to carry out this part of the work.

However, Father Pratt died before the church was quite finished. By his wish he was buried in a tomb within the church, and it was intended to adorn this tomb with his effigy. Myers gave this work, for which he was paid £36, to Thomas Earp, who was described as 'one of Myers' clever assistants' by Charles Hadfield, son of the senior architect.

Working to a death-mask, and careful measurements taken of the deceased priest, Thomas Earp completed the effigy in time for the unveiling and solemn dedication at a High Mass in St Marie's in 1850.

St Marie's was further embellished by Thomas Earp in the form of a deeply carved niche in the outer wall, depicting a highly expressive Annunciation group. As can be seen from the illustration, Mary and the Angel are presented in strikingly lifelike attitudes.

On 1 May 1851, Queen Victoria opened the Great Exhibition in Paxton's famous Crystal Palace in Hyde Park. The idea behind the Exhibition originated with the Annual Exhibition of the Society of Arts. Henry Cole, a civil servant, proposed the scheme to the Society's President, Prince Albert, a keen patron of arts and sciences. Paxton's design for a glass-and-girder exhibition building was accepted after many other designs had been rejected by a Building Committee which included Sir Charles Barry and I.K. Brunel, (of GWR fame). The Crystal Palace was put up in nine months, unlike the Houses of Parliament, which took twenty-five years and was still a-building. It stood along the south side of Hyde Park.

The interior features included a medieval court, designed by Pugin to house examples of decorative sculpture, ceramics, stained glass, metalwork and glassware — all work by leading craftsmen of the day, both British and foreign. George Myers and his team contributed examples from his workshops, which included an oak cabinet decorated with carvings, an impressive canopied font, and a canopied statue in stone of the Blessed Virgin and Child, intended for one of Pugin's churches.

The exhibition attracted thousands of visitors from home and abroad, and was a meeting-place for architects and their patrons to discuss and criticise the merits of the pieces offered for view. Charles Barry came with his sons, Edward and Charles; George Gilbert Scott found time from his work of restoring cathedrals to come with his brilliant pupils, George Edmund Street and George Frederick Bodley. All were prepared to take note of the work of master-sculptors and carvers, among whom Thomas Earp and his colleagues were most certainly included.

It is not surprising, therefore, that shortly after the Great Exhibition closed, Thomas Earp set up his own works in Cambridge Place, off the Westminster Road in Lambeth. He began executing commissions for many of the architects whose interest had been aroused at the Great Exhibition and who needed sculptors to meet the demand created by the Gothic Revival and the stimulus afforded by the rebuilding of the Palace of Westminster.

His first great patron, Pugin, died in 1852, a victim of the conflict and stress associated with the Great Exhibition and its aftermath. He himself had detested the 'glass-and-girder' creation of Paxton, despite his involvement, and the conflict of ideals affected his reason. His churches stand as a true memorial to his genius and it was at one of them, St Mary's, Derby, that Thomas Earp did work towards its embellishment.

St Mary's was designed by Pugin and had been opened in 1837. Dr Nicholas Wiseman called it 'without exception the most magnificent thing Catholics have yet done in modern times in this country'. Anglican Rev Basil Clarke, the excellent church art historian, however, describes it as a 'Gothic goose' for some reason best known to himself. The church was extended in 1853 by a Lady Chapel designed by J.A. Hansom, who gave his name to the Hansom cab. To complete the decoration of the Lady Chapel, Thomas Earp was commissioned to carve a 'Pieta' to designs by Mr John Powell. It is a piece in mezzo-relief, depicting the dead Christ lying in the arms of the grieving Blessed Virgin. Draperies and contours flow in a classical style, and the group also includes St John, Mary Magdalen and two angels. Comparison with the 'Pieta' of Michelangelo in Rome is interesting. The Rome 'Pieta' is modelled in strict proportion and, as a consequence, does not conform with realism in that Christ appears much smaller than his Mother who, if standing, would have been about eight feet tall. The designer of the Derby 'Pieta' appears to have aimed at more realism, for the relative sizes of Christ and the Virgin are more credible. It is the entablature which gives the work its proportion. It is a beautiful example of Earp's carving.

This sculptured group fills the reredos above the chapel altar. Patronage by wealthy gentry made such integral sculpture, rare in a Catholic church, possible. Later on in the century financial considerations obliged Catholic parishes to rely more on mass-produced movable images as objects of devotion, and Earp's works in places of Catholic worship got fewer as time went on.

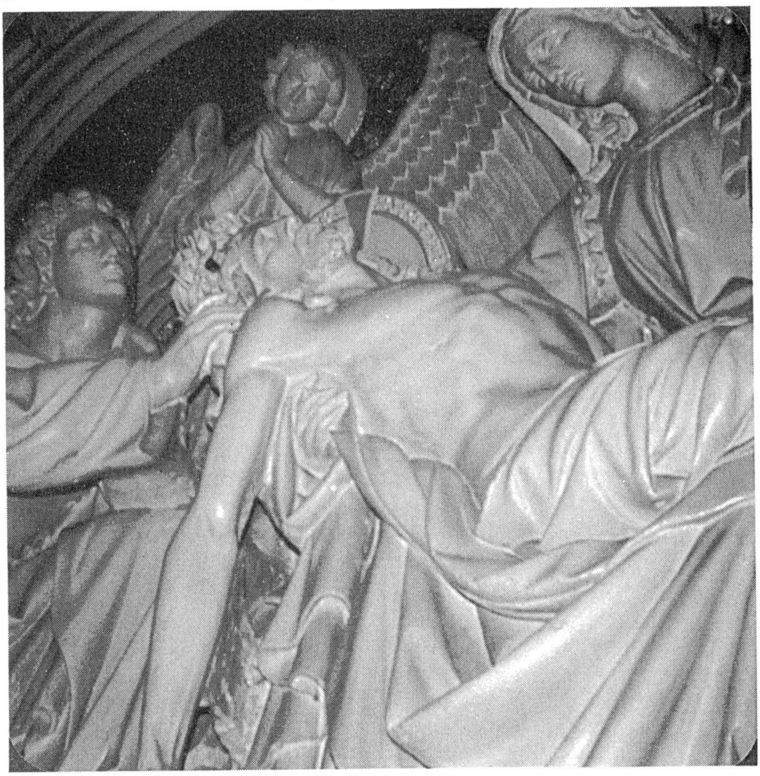

St Mary's Church, Derby: the 'Pieta'.

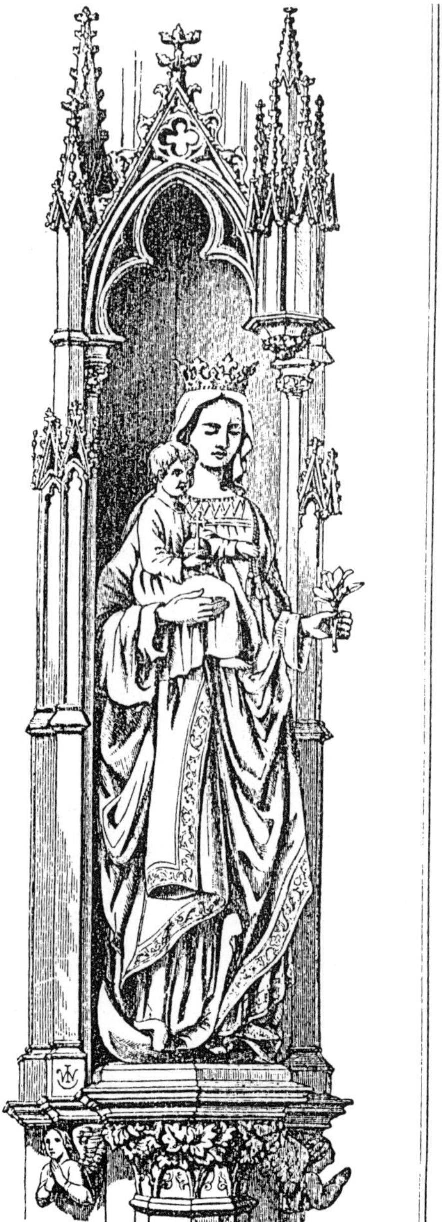

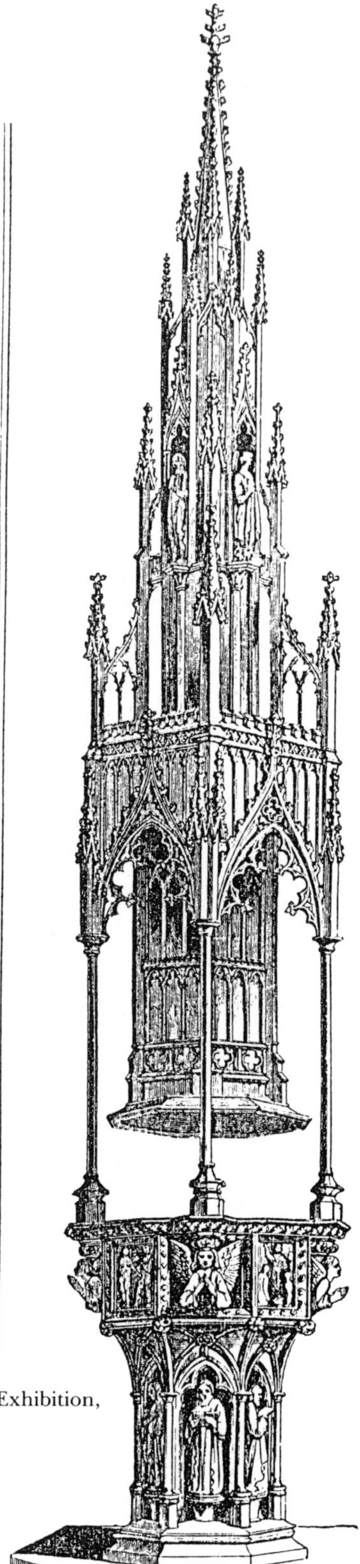

Work of George Myers' craftsmen at Great Exhibition, 1851. (RIBA)

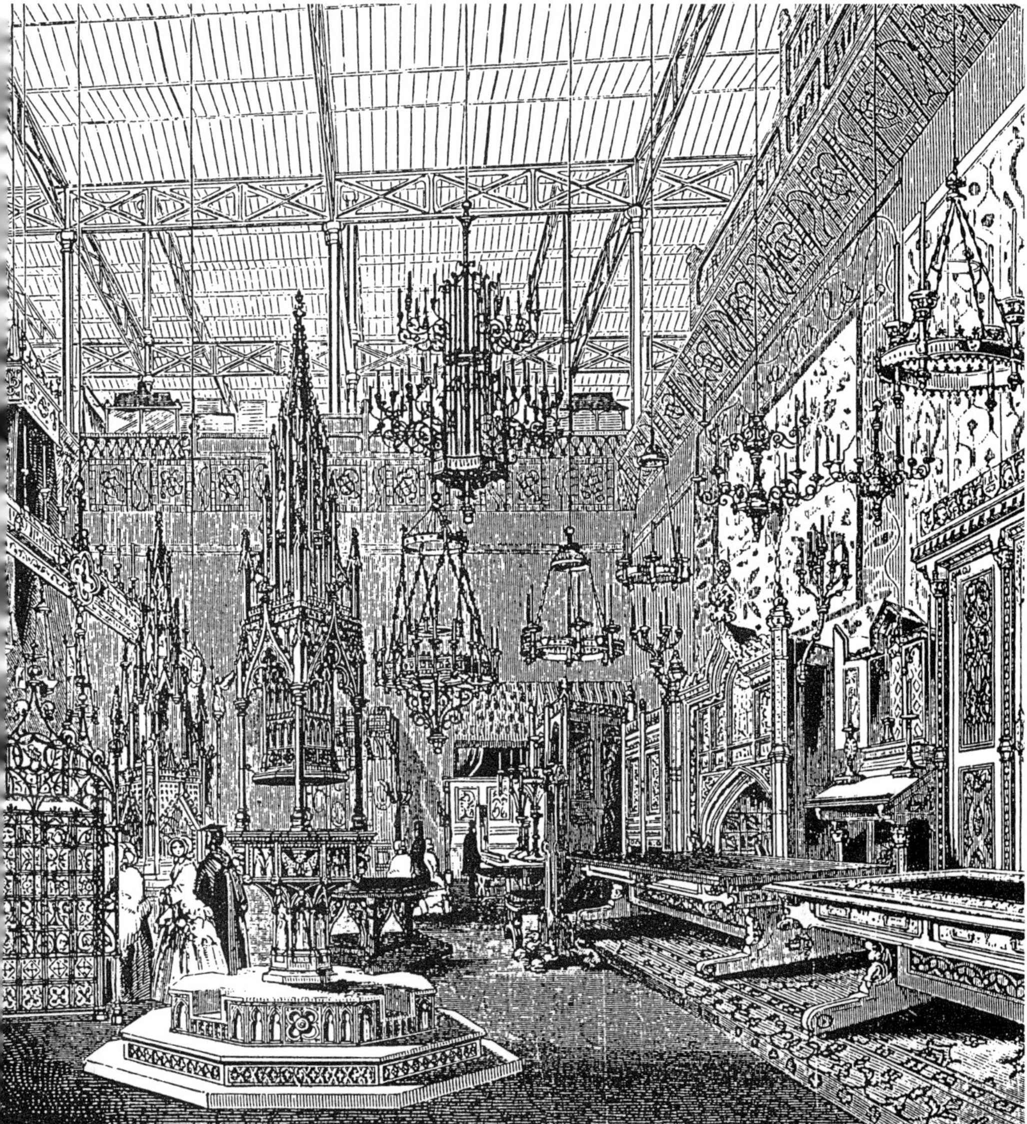

Medieval court, Great Exhibition, 1851. (RIBA)

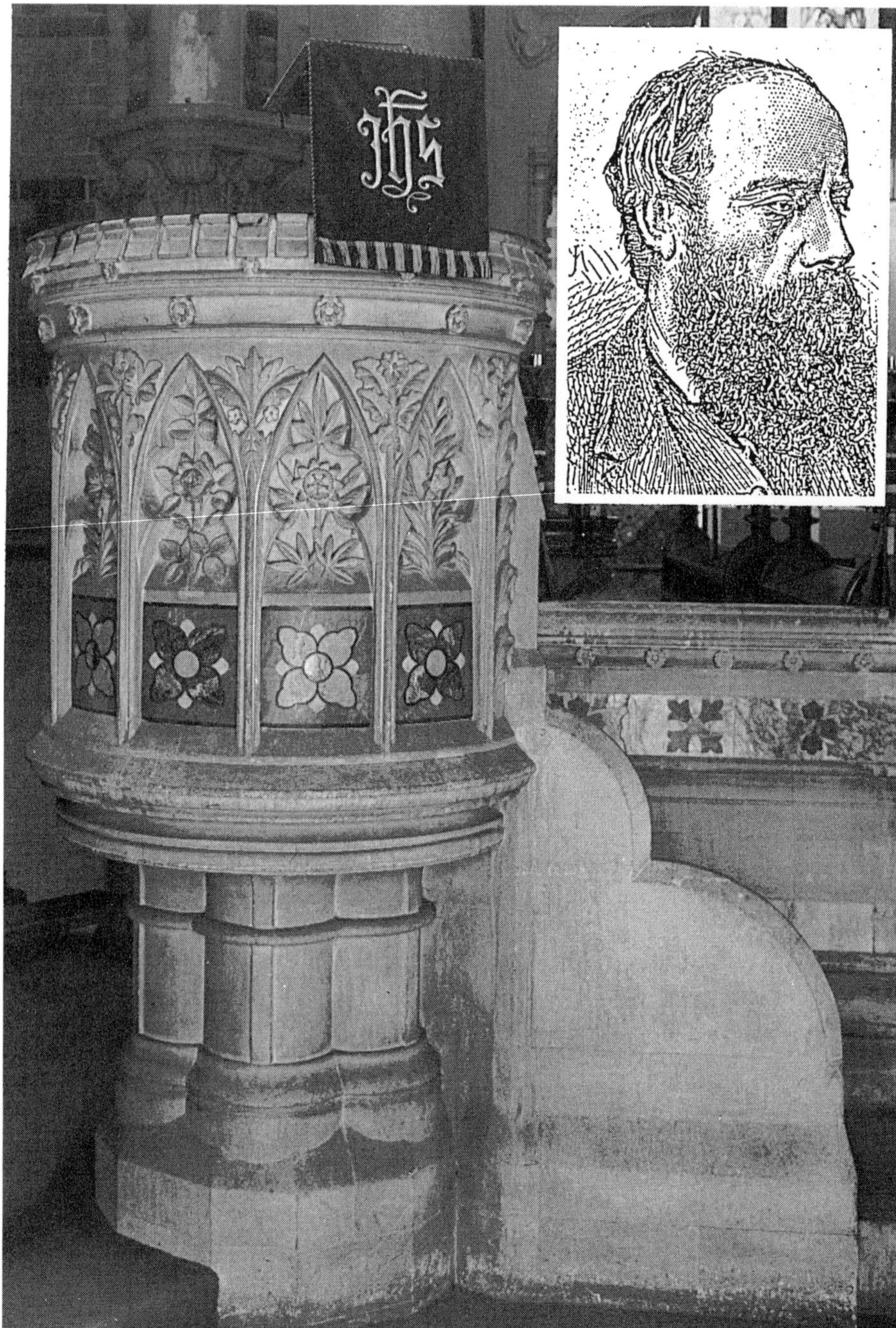

ABOVE: All Saints, Boyne Hill, Maidenhead: pulpit. (NMR) INSET: George Edmund Street. (RIBA)

PLEASING DESIGNS

After the death of Pugin much of Thomas Earp's patronage stemmed from Sir Gilbert Scott's studios at No 20 Spring Gardens, London. Scott until 1845 had been in partnership with W.B. Moffatt, the son of a builder. This partnership was now dissolved and he became interested in the principles of Gothic art through contacts with the Camden Cambridge Society (later called the Ecclesiological Society) and the writings of Pugin, to whom he had been introduced by George Myers. Scott had already designed many churches, but was unpopular with the Ecclesiological Society for designing a Lutheran church in Germany. In 1847 he obtained his first appointment as a restorer of cathedrals, at Ely, and by the 1850s this led to a commission for work at Lichfield Cathedral.

Trainee architects in his office included George Edmund Street and George Frederick Bodley. From these Thomas Earp received many assignments, in the face of competition from other decorative sculptors of the same calibre, such as Farmer and Brindley and Harry Hems, all London-based, and Theodore Phyffers, the Belgian carver Pugin brought over to assist in the interior decoration of the Palace of Westminster.

Earp's output developed through a need for ornamental work such as bosses, finials, corbels, crockets, and for the provision of embellished pulpits, fonts, reredoses for altar-pieces, and capitals for pillars. From an early date a satisfactory partnership developed between himself and Street.

George Edmund Street had been a solicitor's son and was brought up and educated in Camberwell, the district next to Lambeth, where Charles Barry originally had his offices. Street did not wish to follow his father's profession, and began to study architecture under Owen Brown Carter. Such was his progress that in 1845 he became a member of the Ecclesiological Society. This, together with his personal leanings towards High Churchmanship, which favoured ritual and the greater use of outward show and decoration in the expression of worship, called for highly skilled and dedicated assistants for the execution of his designs, and Thomas Earp was foremost among those he regarded with favour.

Scott found Street such a valuable coadjutator in his restorative work that he gave him the opportunity of starting an independent practice while still his nominal assistant.

Street's first commission was the church at Biscovey, in Cornwall. By 1850, having almost a score of churches and schools to his credit, he was appointed by Samuel Wilberforce to be the honorary diocesan architect of Oxford. Under this patronage he designed the church of All Saints, Boyne Hill, Maidenhead, which was built between 1854 and 1857. The *Ecclesiologist* wrote in 1854: 'The style is an ornate Geometrical Middle Pointed'. The inside of the church was made of red and blue brick, and Thomas Earp did the carving of the stone pulpit and the low stone screen, and also scenes of the Passion in mezzo-relief along the walls. Again, to quote the *Ecclesiologist:* 'We have seldom been more pleased with a design than the one before us'.

Another result of the early Street-Earp partnership was at St Paul's Church, Camberwell. Street employed Thomas Earp to carve the reredos and the nave capitals. The reredos, or altar-piece, is of reddish polished alabaster and marble. There is a roundel in the centre with a cruciform symbol. Flanking this, the four Gospel-writers are peeping out of round openings, and on each side of the centre panel are two pillars topped by elaborate acroterions, supporting an entableture richly carved in a foliage pattern, in the typical medieval style in which Earp was most successful.

In 1859 Mr Street was presented with £500 by the Misses Monk, daughters of the Bishop of Gloucester, for the building of a new church in memory of their father. It was to be sited in Pimlico, by what is now known as Vauxhall Bridge Road. Street intended to follow the example of William Butterfield's church at Margaret Street, where brick was used as a basic material instead of the traditional stone. London had become a brick city and bricks were cheap and durable. Decoration was achieved by the use of bands of different colours. The contractor was George Myers. This church was dedicated to St James the Less.

Being a High Churchman, Street designed this church on Tractarian principles and so made the high altar the focus of attention, and it is without a screen. Over the chancel arch is a fresco by G.F. Watts, and the stained-glass windows are by Clayton and Bell, all carried out under Street's supervision. The decorative stone carving of the capitals and the pulpit was divided between Pearce and Earp, Pearce performing most of it and Earp doing the pulpit. The pulpit itself is a prominent and massive piece, covered with elaborately-carved figurework. It has not worn well in London's damp. The church is noted for its almost free-standing tower and the ironwork of the outdoor railings are of outstanding merit.

Street and Earp also entered an interesting collaboration with Scott for restoration work in Lichfield Cathedral. Here Street designed a tomb for Archdeacon Hodson, one of the co-founders of the Lichfield Diocesan Society. The *Building News* of 9 January

1857 said this about Hodson's tomb, when it was still on view at a preliminary exhibition: 'It consists... of an unfinished monument in Caen Stone, to be fixed on the southern side of Lichfield Cathedral to the memory of Archdeacon Hodson...This work is designed by Mr. Street, the architect, and is executed by Mr. Thomas Earp, the figure and general ornamental wood and stone carver, of Cambridge Place, Westminster Road, Lambeth'. The report went on to describe the monument, which consisted of two recessed arches supported by polished Lizard serpentine pillars with elaborate capitals. The arches, when the monument was completed and installed, enframed representations of the Crucifixion and Ascension. Two further recesses underneath contained carvings depicting the Entombment and Resurrection in white Staffordshire alabaster. The report ended: 'This tomb is designed and worked out in the true medieval spirit of the late Early English period, and reflects great credit both on the architect and sculptor'.

Who was the dignitary who merited commemoration on such a scale? Archdeacon Hodson, besides being a co-founder of the Diocesan Society, was trustee of livings for the diocese. He had written a book entitled *The Danger of Receding from the Principles of the Protestant Reformation.* He was also an advocate of better pay for school teachers.

Lichfield Cathedral contains another tomb, erected some years later on the other side of the aisle, for the Archdeacon's nephew, Major Hodson, killed at Lucknow during the Indian mutiny. It displays in bold relief scenes of the battle, carved by Thomas Earp, picturing the luckless man lying prostrate from his wounds. An interesting comment is made by Pevsner in his own monumental work: he calls it 'showy and restless, heralding today's brutalism'.

The adornment of tombs was a route by which Thomas Earp carved his way into the favourable notice of the architects of the day. People of substance ordered elaborate monuments, not only as a way of assuaging their grief, but also to symbolise their hopes for a life hereafter, in a form acceptable to those for whom praying for the dead may have smacked too much of medieval superstition. It was also a way of reasserting their beliefs in things supernatural at a time when traditional beliefs were being challenged by the findings of science. The *Origin of Species* was published towards the end of that decade.

Thus, in 1858 Edward Middleton Barry designed a monstrous tomb to Alexander Berens, and Thomas Earp carved the external statuary, consisting of the four evangelists standing at the corners, and scenes from the New Testament along its sides. It is situated in the great cemetery at West Norwood, and stands on one of its highest knolls. Today it is much the worse for a century of bad weather and neglect: a tree grows out of the middle.

It has, however, survived another monument of that decade that stood a mile away on neighbouring Sydenham Hill — Paxton's Crystal Palace, enlarged and modified after transfer from Hyde Park.

Another tomb featuring sculpture by Thomas Earp was set up in 1854 to a certain Chancellor Raikes, in the Old Cemetery at Chester.

The growing independence of Thomas Earp as a tradesman is indicated by the commissions he received from patrons other than Scott or Street. Edward Barry offered him considerable patronage during this decade and beyond. For one of his earliest works, St Saviour's at South Hampstead, Thomas Earp provided the carved pulpit and reredos, both featuring statuary in Gothic-style embellished arches. This church, situated near the foot of Haverstock Hill, which rises just north of Chalk Farm, was opened in 1856.

Thomas Earp was offered a commission to decorate the interior of the church of St John the Baptist at France Lynch, Gloucestershire, by Street's fellow-associate, George Bodley. For this Earp had to travel to the Cotswolds in 1858 to carve, *in situ*, the angels playing musical instruments that adorn the upper part of the nave, and the Annunciation motifs in the corbels. It was excellent work.

Meanwhile Joseph Hansom, still carrying out commissions from Roman Catholic sources, built the church of St David at Dalkeith, according to the desires of Lady Cecil, the Dowager Marchioness of Lothian, a recent convert to Catholicism. Thomas Earp carved the altar-piece with quatrefoil reliefs of Our Lady, St Margaret and of St David. The church itself, which was dedicated in 1854, has come to be regarded as one of the outstanding buildings of its kind in the country, and a good example of Hansom's work. The altar-piece has survived alteration occasioned by ritualistic changes in recent years, and Thomas Earp's carvings, as far as can be ascertained, are untouched; I found them striking.

Street was by now firmly established as Oxford's diocesan architect, and Thomas Earp was employed in carrying out several of his designs, notably the memorial fountain to Eliza Marshall in the churchyard of St Kenelm's, Enstone, and the medieval cross in the churchyard of St Mary's, Iffley. In Oxford city itself, Street designed the church of St Philip and St James, intended to be the parish church for North Oxford; it was an ambitious project, built in 1861-2. Thomas Earp's workshops supplied the elaborately carved capitals in the nave, the finials, the sedilia, and the reredos. The subject of the reredos carvings was first intended to be the Crucifixion, but this was too much for the genteel worshippers of North Oxford to behold. The design was then altered to the less harrowing (for the beholder) Agony in the Garden. This reredos was altered afterwards to Street's suggestions, being raised, reframed, coloured and gilded by Messrs Burlison and Grylls. Charles Eastlake wrote 'The rich inlay and carving of the reredos (heightened in effect by contrast with the plain wall lining and simple wood fittings of the chancel) are all full of character'.

Thomas Earp's work under Street was by no means confined to Oxford. Restoration work at St Mary's Church, Stone, Kent included a new pulpit donated by the family of Archdeacon Walter King. Under Street's direction Thomas Earp carved recessed arches on the outside of the pulpit but, presumably because of ritualistic prejudices, these arches were left unadorned by figures.

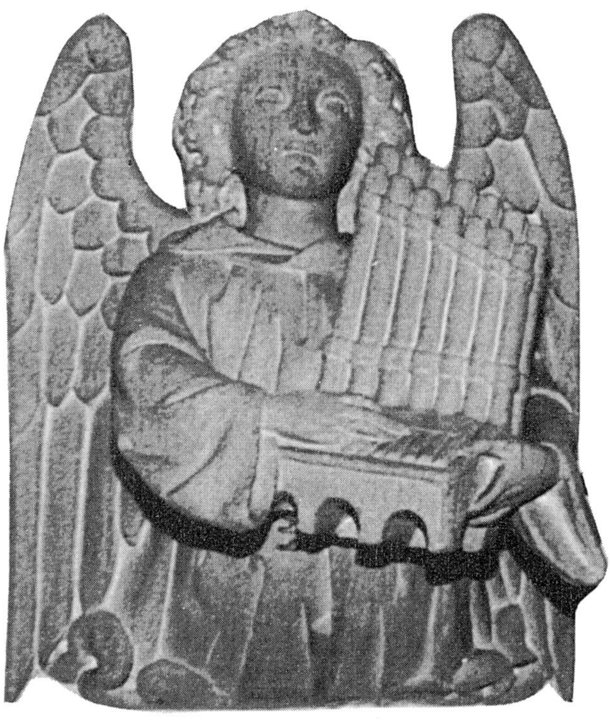

St John the Baptist, France Lynch: musical angel motif. (PM)

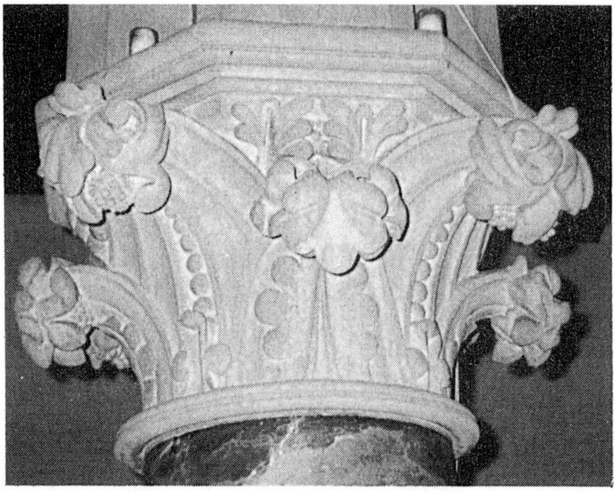

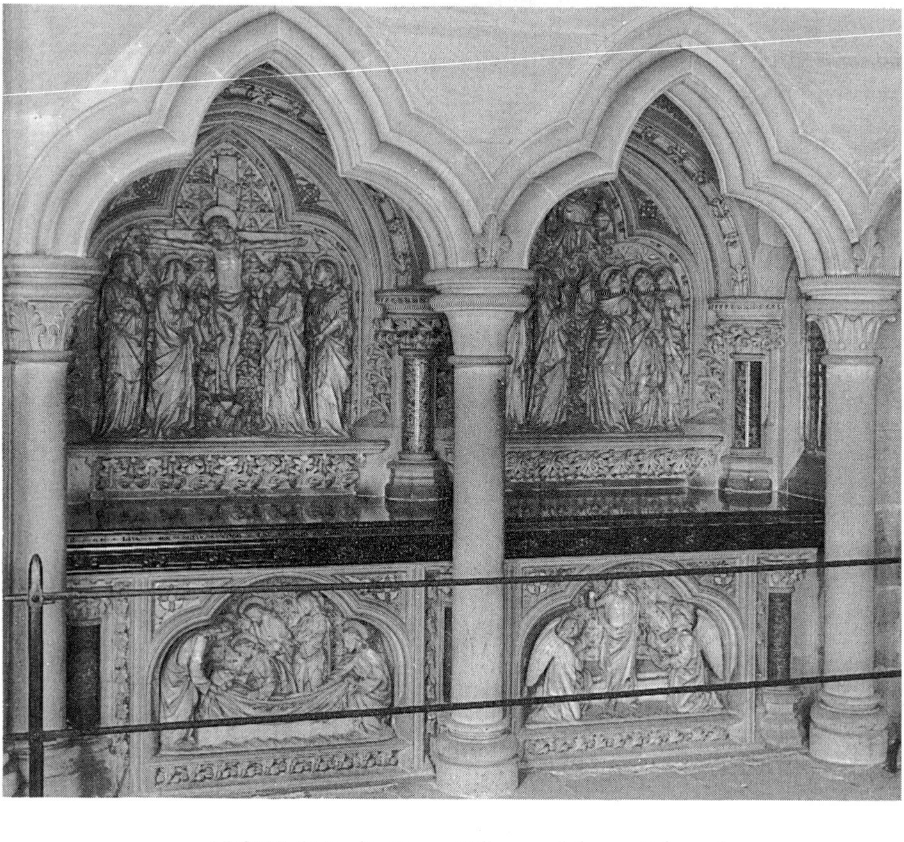

ABOVE: St Paul's, Herne Hill: one of the capitals on the nave pillars. BELOW: Lichfield Cathedral: monument to Archdeacon Hodson. (NMR)

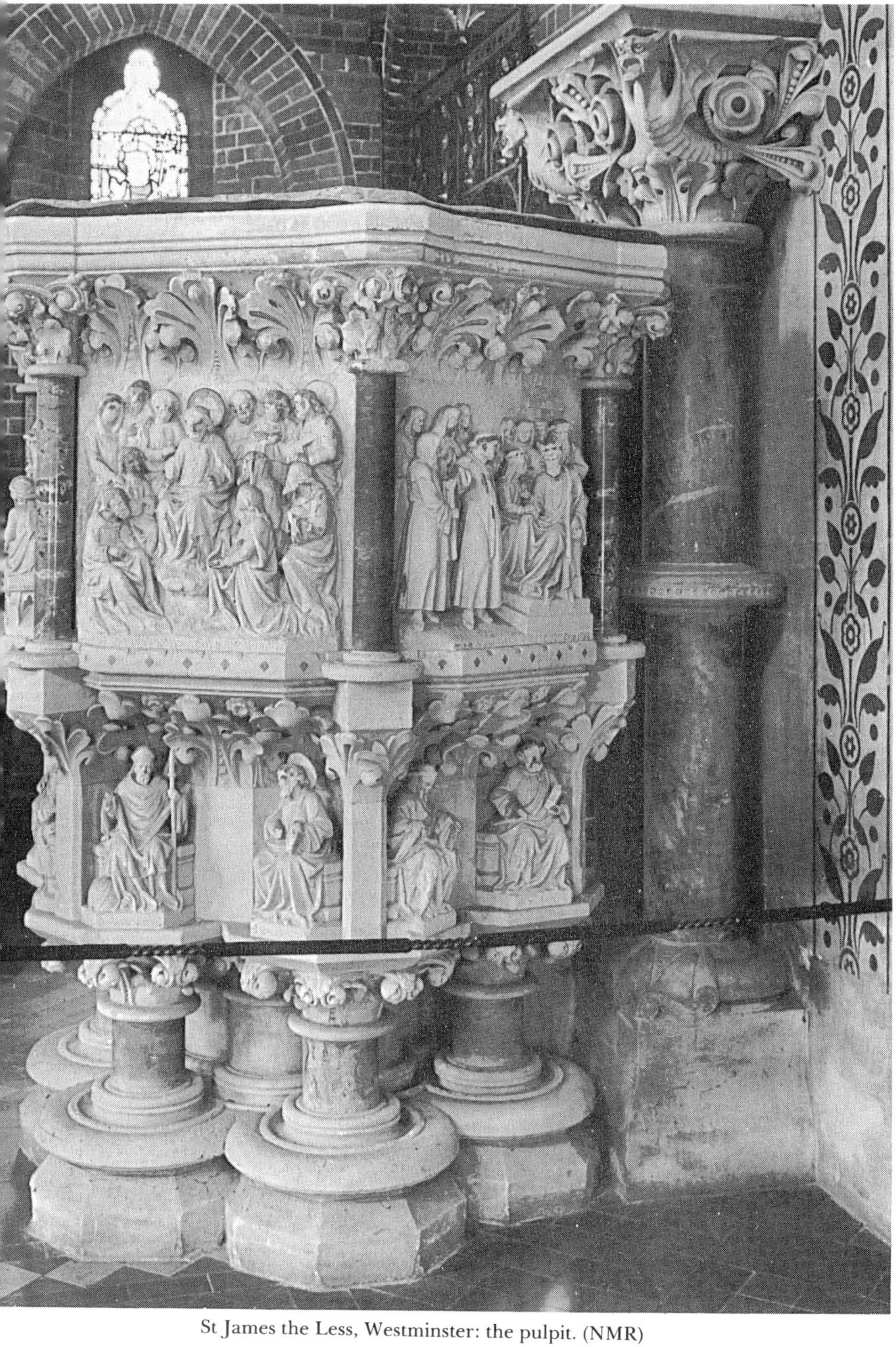

St James the Less, Westminster: the pulpit. (NMR)

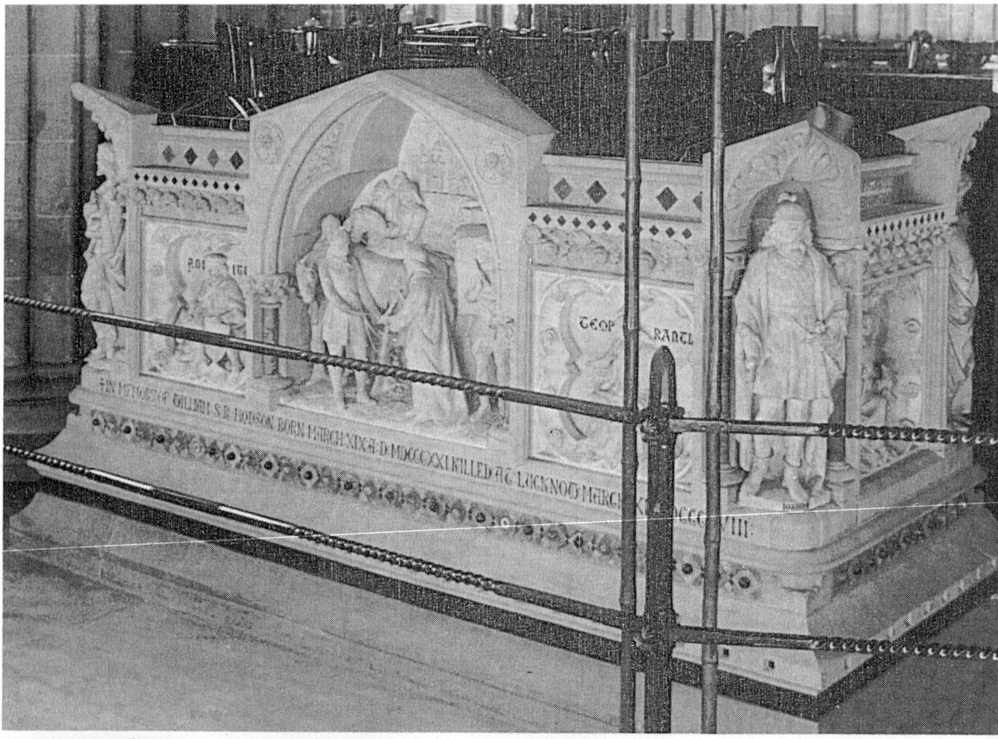

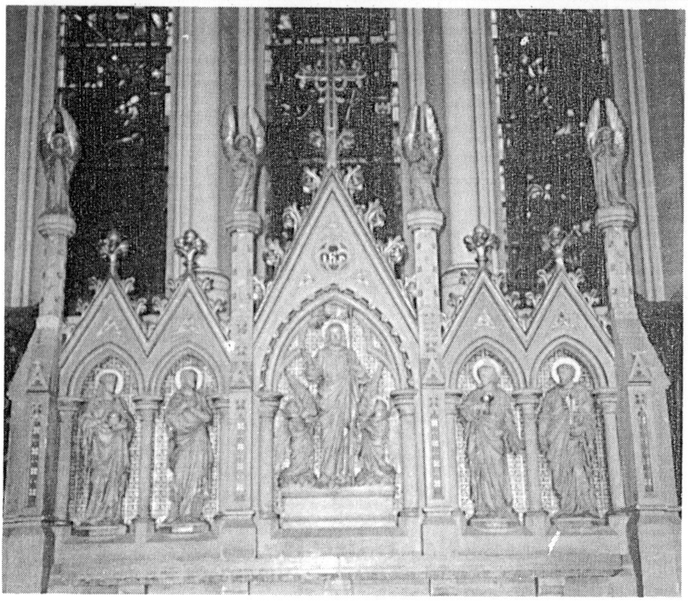

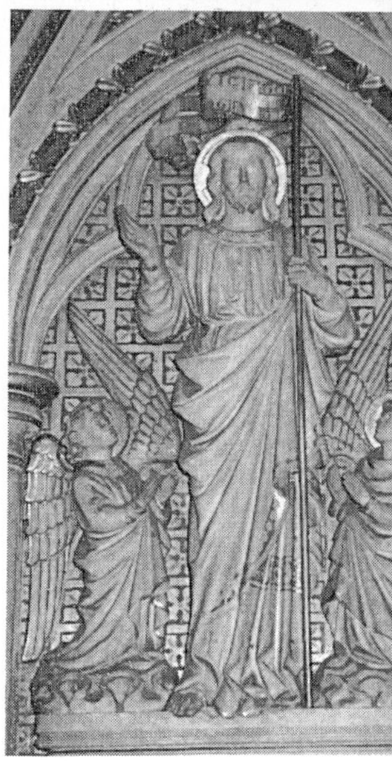

ABOVE: Lichfield Cathedral: monument to Major Hodson. (NMR) LEFT: St Saviour's Church, South Hampstead: reredos and RIGHT: detail. (Both DCN-S)

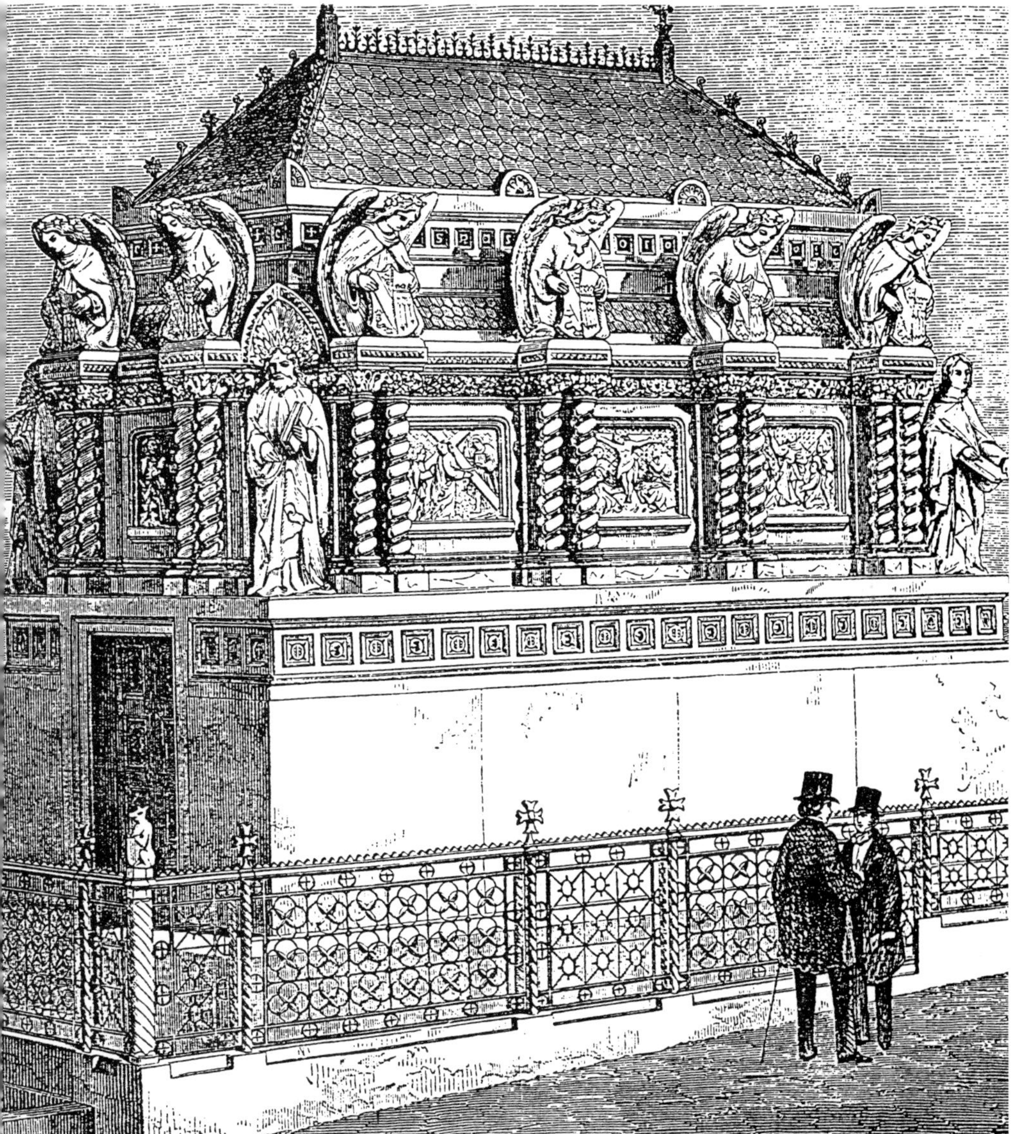

The tomb for Mr Berens, West Norwood Cemetery, London. (RIBA)

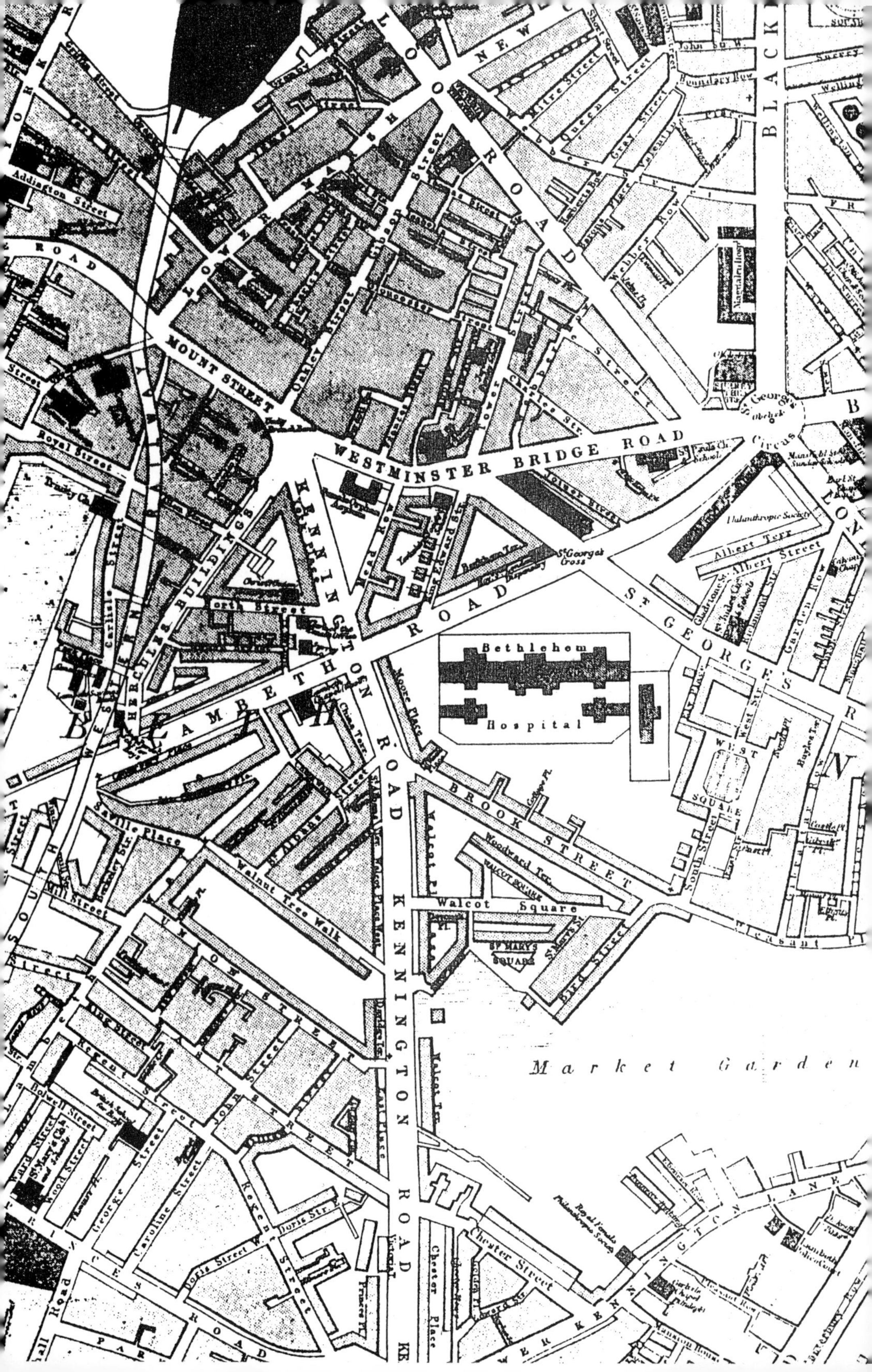
WESTMINSTER BRIDGE ROAD
LAMBETH ROAD
KENNINGTON ROAD
ST GEORGE'S ROAD
BROOK STREET
MOUNT STREET
Bethlehem Hospital
Walcot Square
Walnut Tree Walk
Saville Place
Mill Street
UNION STREET
Royal Street
Addington Street
HERCULES BUILDINGS
Albert Street
Philanthropic Society
WEST SQUARE
South Street
Market Garden
Chester Street
Kennington Lane
Westminster Bridge Road
St. George's Circus
Gloucester Street
Oakley Street
St. Mary's Square
Bird Street
Charles Street
Queen Street
Mitre Street
Short Street
John St.
Surrey
Webber Row
Gray Street
Boundary Row
Woodward Ter.
Walcot Place
Moore Place
Regent Street
King Street
George Street
Caroline Street
Doris Street
Kennington Road
Chester Place
Royal Female Philanthropic Society
Bolwell Street
Ward Street
Wood Street

Map of North Lambeth, c1870. (GLC)

Life and Work in London

The volume of work flowing from the Earp workshops involved a complex establishment of staff and processes.

A census return of 1861 suggests that, by this time, Thomas Earp employed twenty-one men and eight apprentices. He had moved from Hercules Buildings, and his workshops were removed from Cambridge Place to what is now called the Kennington Road, in those days variously named Wolsingham or York Place. The houses in the area had mostly been erected about 1790 on part of the copyhold land of the Archbishop of Canterbury. The actual home of the Earp family, for a time at least, was in Mead Row, a turning off the Kennington Road almost adjoining the Earp workshops, with a police station between. With Thomas and Isabella, and their three children, Isabella Caroline, Edith Florence, and Arthur Clifford, there also lived Thomas's sister Emma, working at her trade of dressmaker to the wealthy wives of West End merchants. An elderly servant named Mary Storey completed the household.

Thomas Earp Senior of Nottingham had joined his son in 1860, following the death of his wife. The older man had taken over the premises at Cambridge Place as a wood-carver. Later he moved into Little Canterbury Place, off the Lambeth Walk.

It is not clear whether the old man developed the craft of wood-carver after abandoning the business of lace- or starch-agent (for which there could have been little scope in London), or whether this craft had always been one of his skills, acquired in his boyhood at Kings Newton and which he had never lost even while employed in the lace industry.

One of Thomas's brothers, Henry, had also come down to London to follow the trade of carver, sometimes working with him and later from his own place of business in Clerkenwell. A carved pulpit in St Mary's Church, Martham, Norfolk, is attributed to Henry Earp, according to a report in an issue of the *Builder* for 1861. Alexander, the youngest brother, had gone into the printing trade, was married and living in Southwark.

Within walking distance of the Earps' home was the Lambeth School of Art. This had been founded by the vicar of St Mary, Lambeth and was already producing trained painters, modellers and decorative carvers. Thomas Earp may well have procured a place there for his son, Arthur, against the time when he would be old enough to learn a trade. One of its directors was John Sparkes, who believed in employing women but not foreigners. He is reported to have said: 'English hands are as skilful as other peoples'...but still French modellers make Stafford pottery... Germans are filling our drawing offices all over the country'. Perhaps with Theodore Phyffers in mind, he fulminated 'Belgian carvers are cutting Romanism into Protestant pulpits'.

Artisans from Lambeth were likely to have gone to work on Scott's new India Office building in Whitehall (now the Foreign and Commonwealth Office), built to the designs he was obliged to adopt due to Palmerston's rejection of a Gothic structure. Thomas Earp himself was responsible for the De La Robbia carving on the frieze surrounding the courtyard at first storey level, blending with and offsetting the work of other sculptors, such as Protat, Nicholls and Phyffers.

The first stage in the execution of a piece of work of decorative sculpture would often be a drawing, done to a design created by the person commissioning the work or his architect or designer. The kind of work done by Earp and his contemporaries would most likely be of this nature, especially that done for Street, who was reputed to be in the habit of designing the small details of his decorative work himself, not countenancing any departures.

A letter in the *Builder* of 18 January 1860 over the signature 'A working carver' may indicate some of the stresses of that calling. It expressed the grief felt by anyone with love and feeling for architecture to find carving carried out in an inartistic manner, and asked why carvers and architects did not work more hand-in-hand. Carvers under pressure were often expected to do their work in half the time needed, and they often lost interest. Carvers were often looked upon as not art-loving, whereas this was often untrue. If they received more confidence and encouragement, the writer of this letter suggested, much more satisfactory work would be produced.

Nevertheless, the relationship between Earp and Street always remained satisfactory, based on the mutual respect both men had for their respective abilities. Sir Gilbert Scott in his autobiography makes the following comment: 'My friend, Mr. Street...has been working on the conventional foliage, Mr. Earp being his handpiece; and he has done very great things'. Street's method of expecting his craftsmen to carry out and execute his designs to the utmost detail had the result of Earp leaving his stamp on the work he did for other architects, even after Street's death.

From the drawing, the sculptor would go on to prepare a model in clay, as near as possible the size of the finished sculpture. Clay being a material liable to shrinkage and crumbling, a mould and cast would be made in some material such as plaster of Paris, which is lighter and more permanent. While in this stage the work would often be presented at exhibitions or for inspection by patrons. From this cast the model would then be copied into the final medium such as marble or alabaster or similar suitable stone.

The type of work that most craftsmen of this category were called upon to do seldom included figures in the round, as in the case of monumental sculpture. It was mostly bas-relief or naturalistic foliage; we can make an exception for prone effigies like those of Father Pratt, or Bishop Pearson or Rowley. It is highly probable that this type of work was carved and chiselled direct into the final material but the use of sketch models in clay or plaster cannot be ruled out.

For carving, a variety of tools would be used. First, a 'pitcher' to knock off corners and angles, resembling a large cold chisel driven with a heavy hammer. Then a 'heavy point' would be used for the main roughing out, followed by a 'fine' point as the final surface was approached. If a model was being used, the method chosen was by means of three compasses, or a pointing instrument. In this case the model would be fixed to one of a pair of 'scalestones', and the block to be hewn on another and, by means of the guidance of a vast number of measuring points, corresponding each one with the other, the piece of stone would be chiselled and rasped to the dimensions and proportions required.

For the refining processes, 'claw' chisels would be employed, working on the stone in all directions. Flat chisels would be used for finishing finer details. Stone gouges, drills, and toothed hammers would be used at the final stages, while rasps, sandpaper and emery cloth would be used to achieve a smooth or polished surface, according to the work to be done. Apprentices would work on the initial stages but, for final completion, the work would be entrusted either to a highly skilled assistant or done by the master sculptor himself, depending on the size and importance of the work.

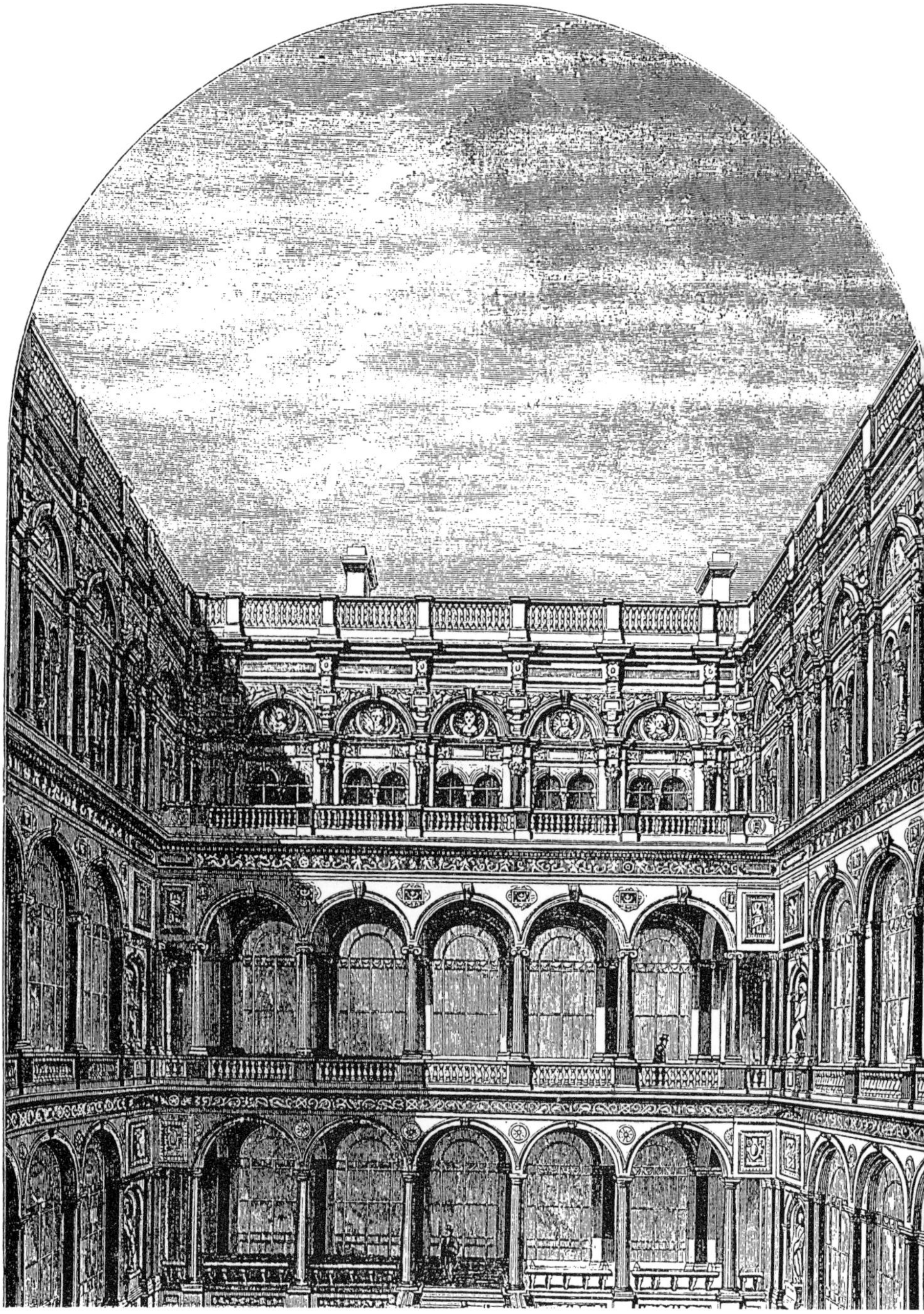

India Office (now Foreign and Commonwealth Office) Whitehall, London: interior courtyard, showing mouldings on upper walls in Della Robbia style. (RIBA)

Graven Images

The Prince Consort died in 1861. To commemorate the Great Exhibition of 1851, and to perpetuate his spirit and work, a London Exhibition of the Works of All Nations was planned for 1862.

To house it a new building was designed by Captain Francis Fowkes, of the Royal Engineers, who also designed the Royal Scottish Museum in Edinburgh. The site chosen was along the Cromwell Road, marking the southern boundary of an area known as the Gore Estate, developed to contain places of culture, learning and research. Fowkes was also associated with the design of the Albert Hall, but died before it was completed.

Glass was not used for this new exhibition building because in 1851 it had been found necessary to use screening to counteract the glare. It was surmounted by domes which were the largest ever built up to that date, 160 feet in diameter, compared with St Paul's 108 feet and the 139 feet of St Peter's, Rome.

Like the one in 1851, the 1862 exhibition also had its medieval court to display works of fine art. About these, the *Building News* of 2 May 1862 made this observation: 'Beneath the gallery of the Medieval Court Earp the carver exhibits some of his best workmanship designed by Mr. Street and Mr. Bentley'.

Thomas Earp's work at the 1862 exhibition included the pulpit, or a model of it, designed for Street's church of St Peter, Bournemouth. This church deserves a description of its own as it is a veritable museum of Thomas Earp's sculptural art.

St Peter's, Bournemouth, was the first commission for a town church undertaken by Street. The first plans, prepared in 1853, were based on an earlier church by Tulloch, and were in accordance with the desires of the then incumbent, Morden Bennett. Both Street and Bennett were in sympathy with the Oxford Movement and the design was envisaged to draw the eye of the worshipper towards the altar, and to provide a setting of suitable and appropriate ornaments and fittings.

The church was not built all at once. Because of the expense, it could only be done by stages over a great period of time. Thomas Earp was responsible for carvings on the font, the reredos, the pulpit, some carvings over an archway in a side aisle, and four statues to ornament the base of the spire.

The pulpit is of inlaid spar and marbles and adorned by a carved angel, bearing a scroll inscribed 'How can they preach, except they be sent'. In the *Memorials of the Rev. J. Keble* by John F. Moor we read the following comments on the Bournemouth church: 'The reredos is exceedingly gorgeous, and exquisitely carved'. This reredos was subsequently painted in colours by Comper, an embellishment which some regarded with mixed feelings. Charles Eastlake remarked that, while the original church had no pretensions to age or architectural excellence, it had been gradually transformed into an interesting example of the Gothic Revival. 'The decorative sculpture of the reredos,' he writes in *The History of the Gothic Revival*, 'is an instance of this architect's fertility of invention in the treatment of detail. No illustration could convey an adequate idea of the beauty and refinement of the carving'. John Keble, main instigator of the Oxford Movement, was among the subscribers to the monument to Bishop Pearson that Earp was to carve for Chester Cathedral in 1863.

The work done for Bentley at the 1862 Exhibition appears to be one of the earliest recorded instances of Earp working for the future architect of Westminster Cathedral. The cusped altar-piece may have been intended to frame a painting by Westlake for the Lady Chapel of the church of St Francis of Assisi in Pottery Lane, North Kensington, designed by Henry Clutton. It can be compared with the reredos carved by Earp for St Margaret's, Lewisham, which also enframes paintings by Westlake.

Also exhibiting in 1862, and laying claim to the services of Thomas Earp, was Samuel Sanders Teulon. Four years earlier, in 1858, an exhibition at the Royal Academy included in its architectural section some drawings by Teulon of his Holy Trinity Church, Hastings, with its wild ground plan, having its corner tower at an angle to the rest of the church. The carvings were executed by Thomas Earp, consisting of a memorial to Dr Crosse, a sculpture group above the organ, and a tympanum over the priest's door. A present-day guide-book *A Church in No-Man's Land*, issued by the incumbent, handsomely describes Earp as 'the greatest living sculptor in the country'. The Royal Academy exhibition also showed Teulon's drawings of additions to Shadwell Court, Norfolk, for which sculptured adornments were executed by Thomas Earp. This Norfolk mansion was built in the Renaissance style, was extended between 1856 and 1860 at the expense of Sir Robert Buxton, and constructed with mainly local materials such as flint, red and white brick, and freestone.

At the 1862 exhibition Teulon put on display the reredos carved by Thomas Earp for the restoration work in the church of St John the Baptist, Huntley, in Gloucestershire. This was done in veined alabaster inlaid with marbles; in the centre panel was the Last

Supper in alabaster, underneath an inlaid mosaic cross. On either side were smaller panels depicting The Rose of Sharon and Lily of the Valley. Crocked pediments on marble shafts topped the structure. The exhibits also included a marble font for St John's.

Teulon was also believed to have regarded Thomas Earp as 'his favourite sculptor' and between them they prepared elaborately carved capitals, spandrels, statuary, altar-pieces, a font and a pulpit. These in their final setting make the interior of St John's a breathtaking display.

Other work at this exhibition, performed by Thomas Earp to Teulon's designs, was a stone drinking fountain which Sir Robert Buxton endowed, to stand in Victoria Tower Gardens, Westminster, to commemorate the abolition of slavery. There was also displayed the alabaster chimney piece that found a home in Elvetham Hall.

Such was the progress made in eleven years. Thomas Earp was no longer one of many assistants to one exhibitor, but a prominent contributor in his own right to the work of several distinguished architects offering their work to public scrutiny.

Captain Fowke's building housing the exhibition was dismantled and part of it used in the construction of the first Alexandra Palace at Muswell Hill. Its Kensington site was afterwards taken for Waterhouse's Natural History Museum. Fowkes's palace did not last long: it was destroyed by fire soon after its erection on Muswell Hill.

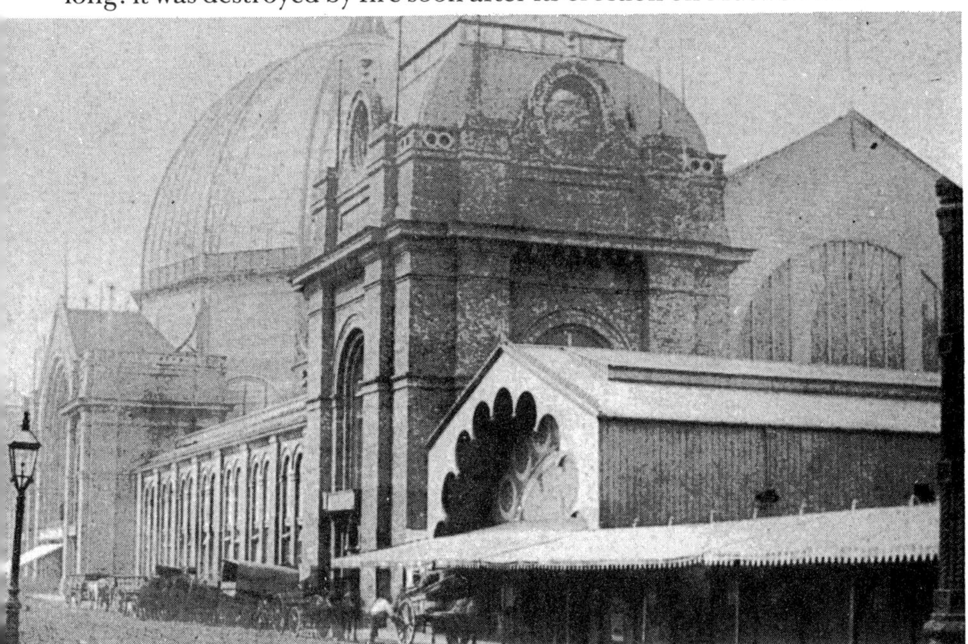

Building for the 1862 Exhibition, Kensington, London.
(NMR)

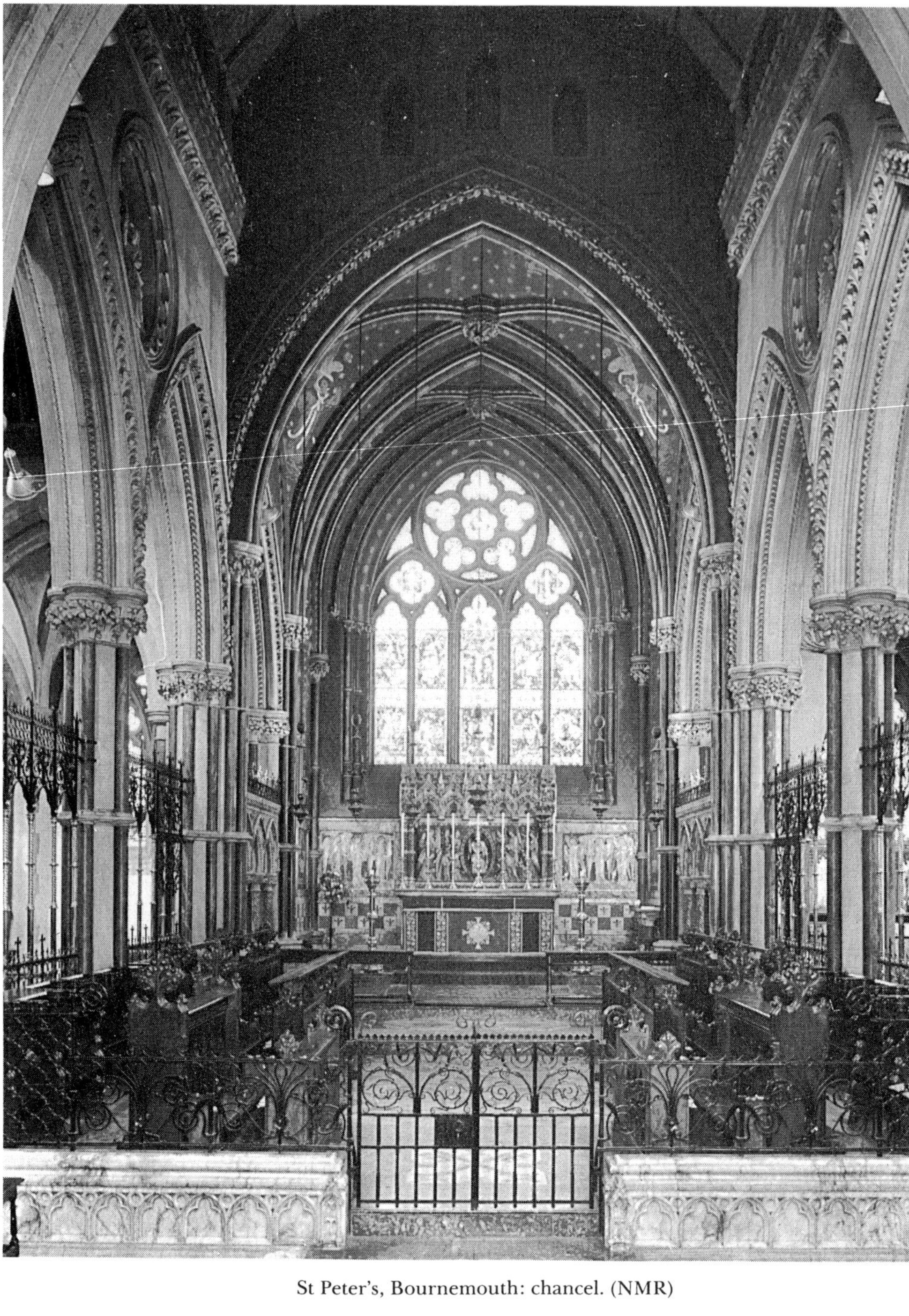

St Peter's, Bournemouth: chancel. (NMR)

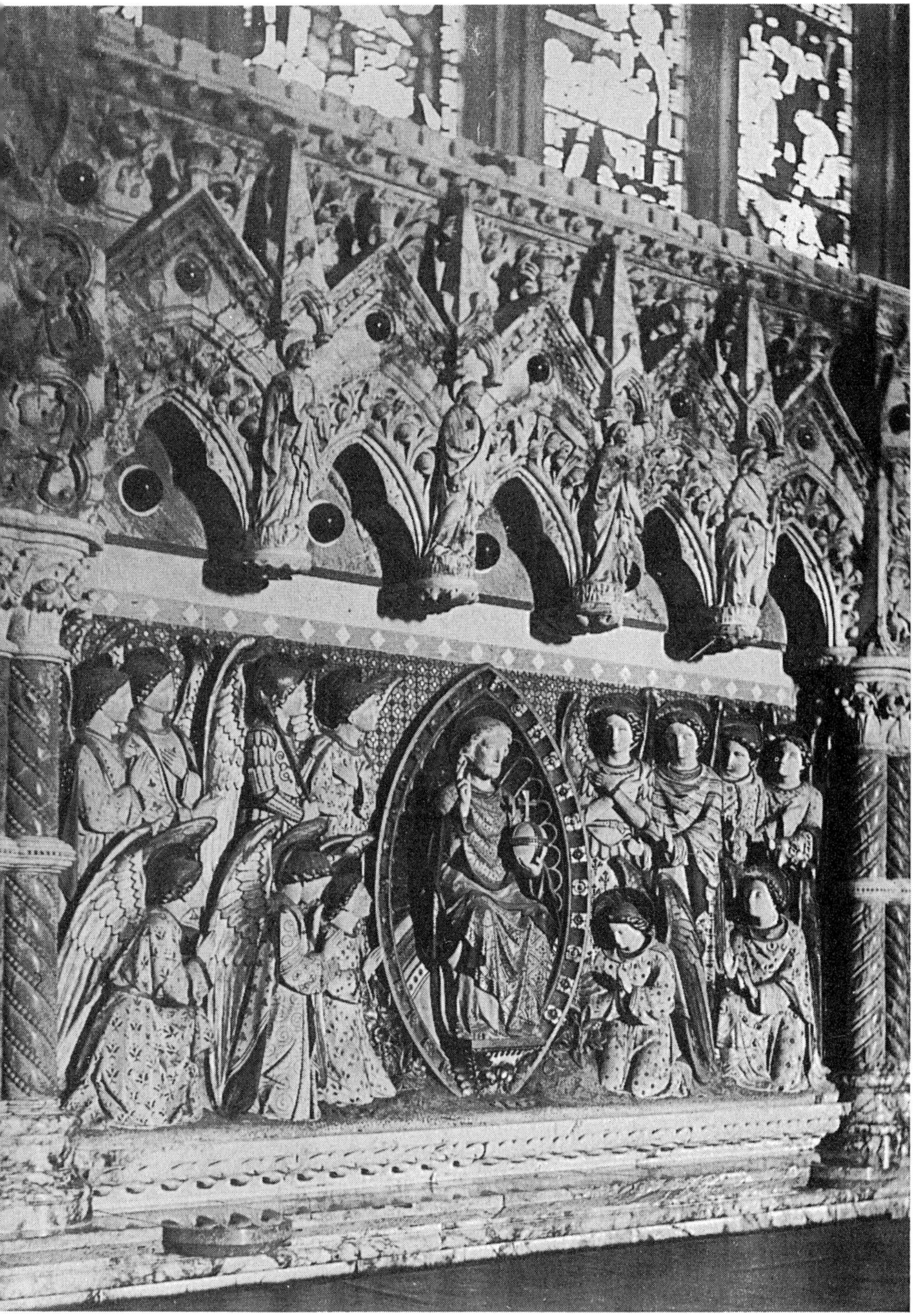

St Peter's, Bournemouth: reredos. (NMR)

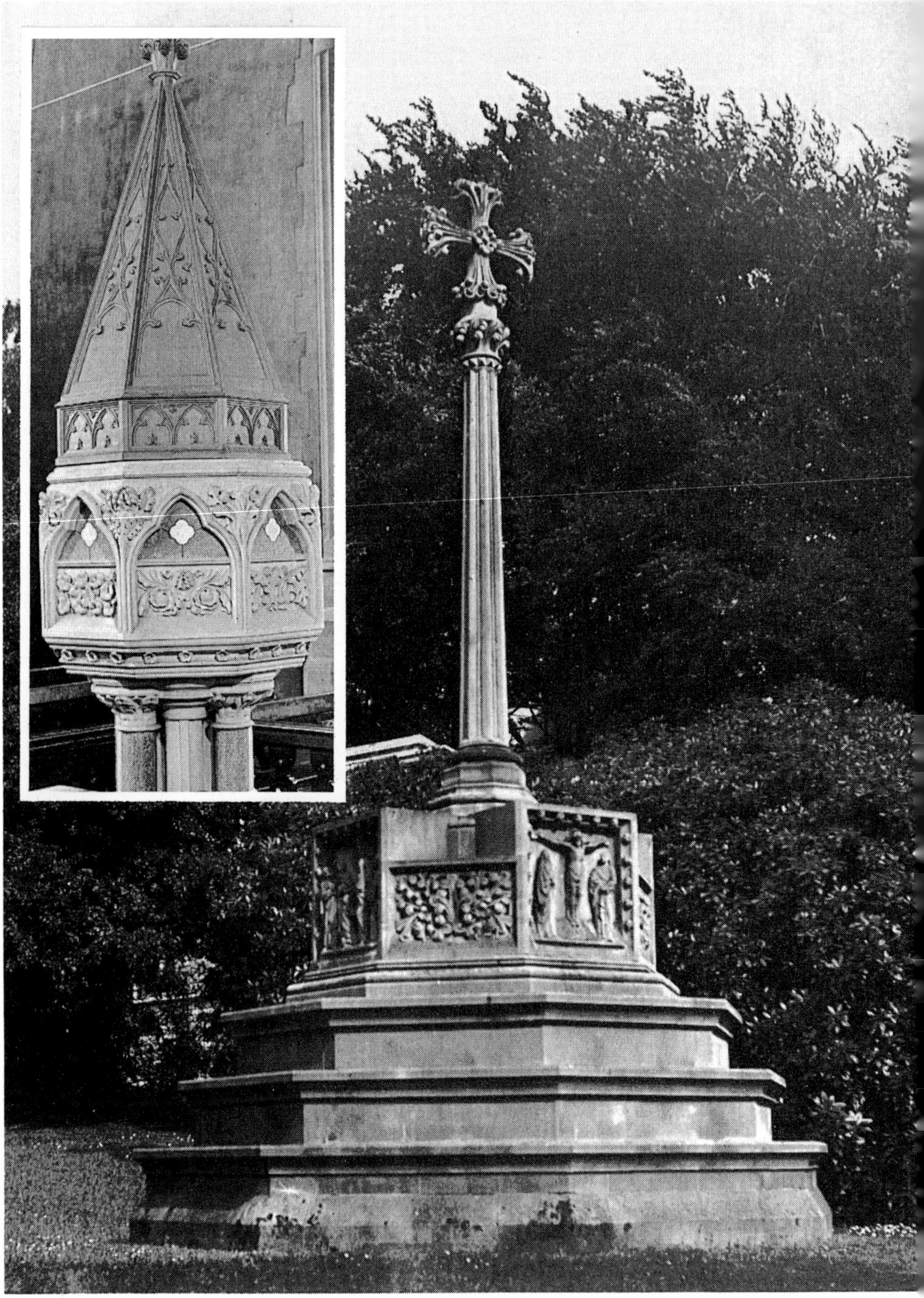

St Peter's, Bournemouth: Memorial Cross and INSET: font. (Both NMR).

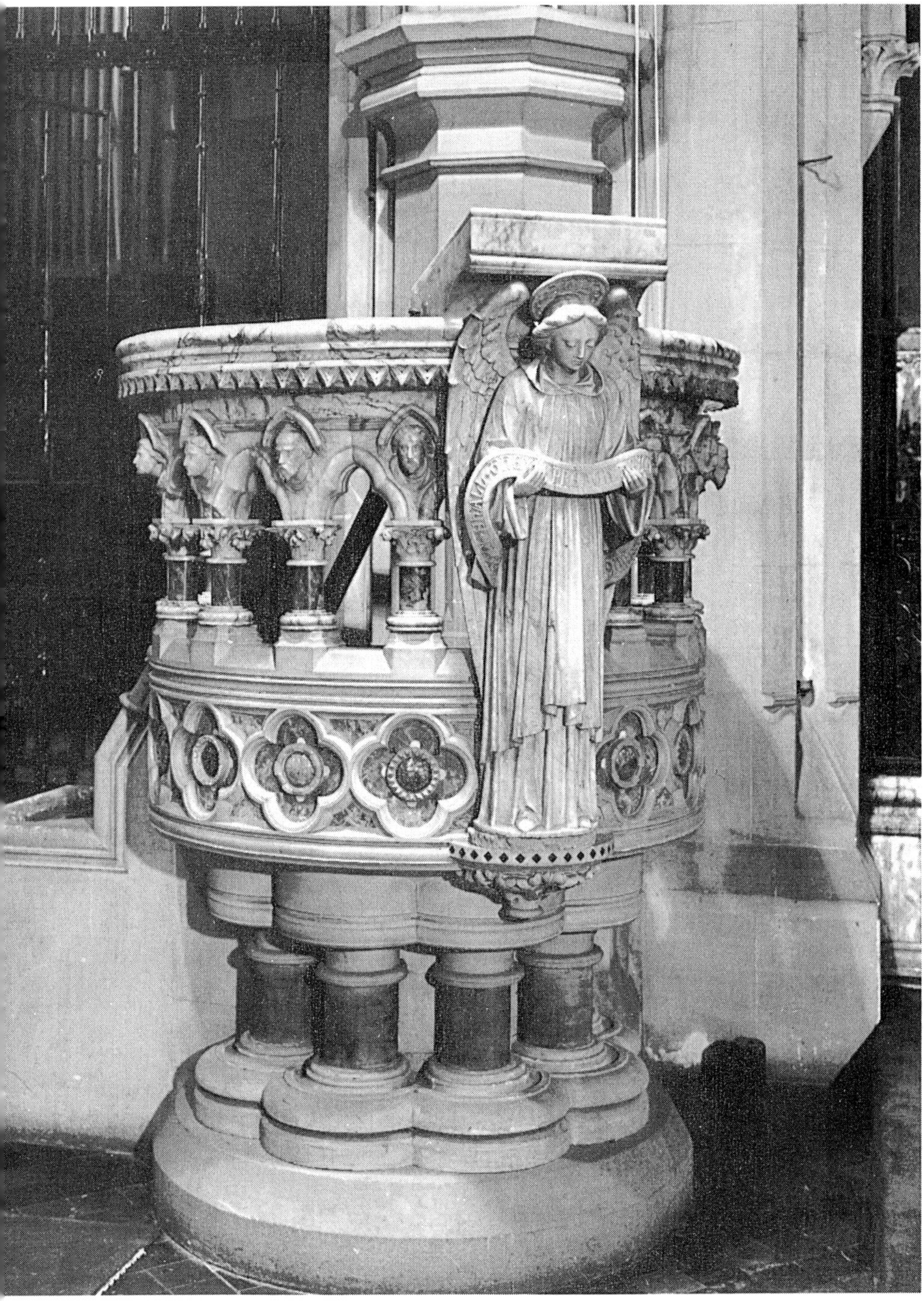

St Peter's, Bournemouth: pulpit. (NMR)

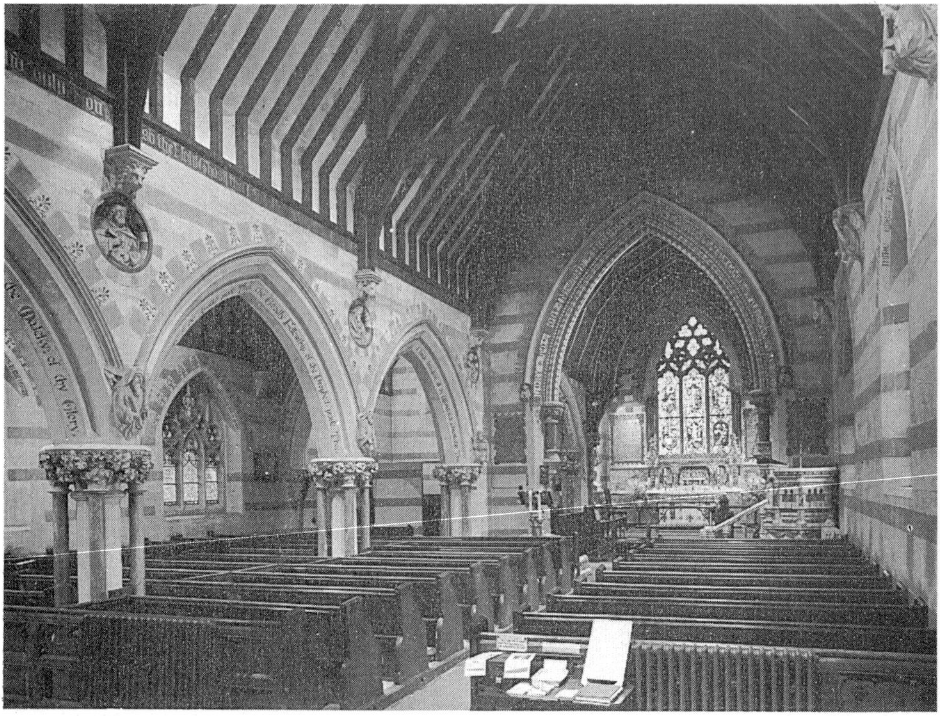

ABOVE: St John the Baptist, Huntley, Glos: the Nave and BELOW: reredos. (Both NMR)

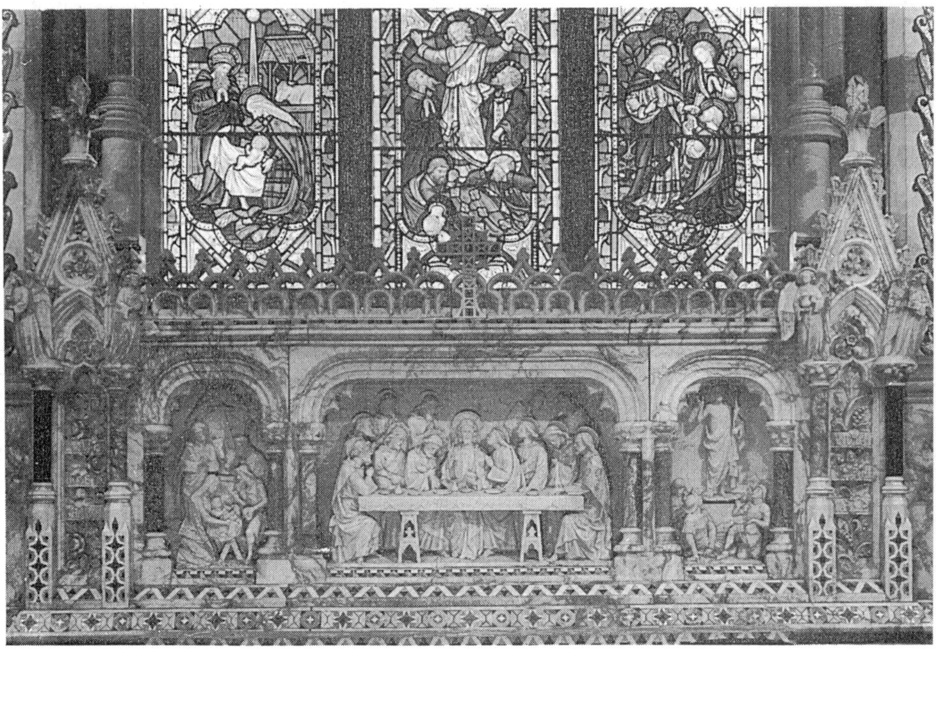

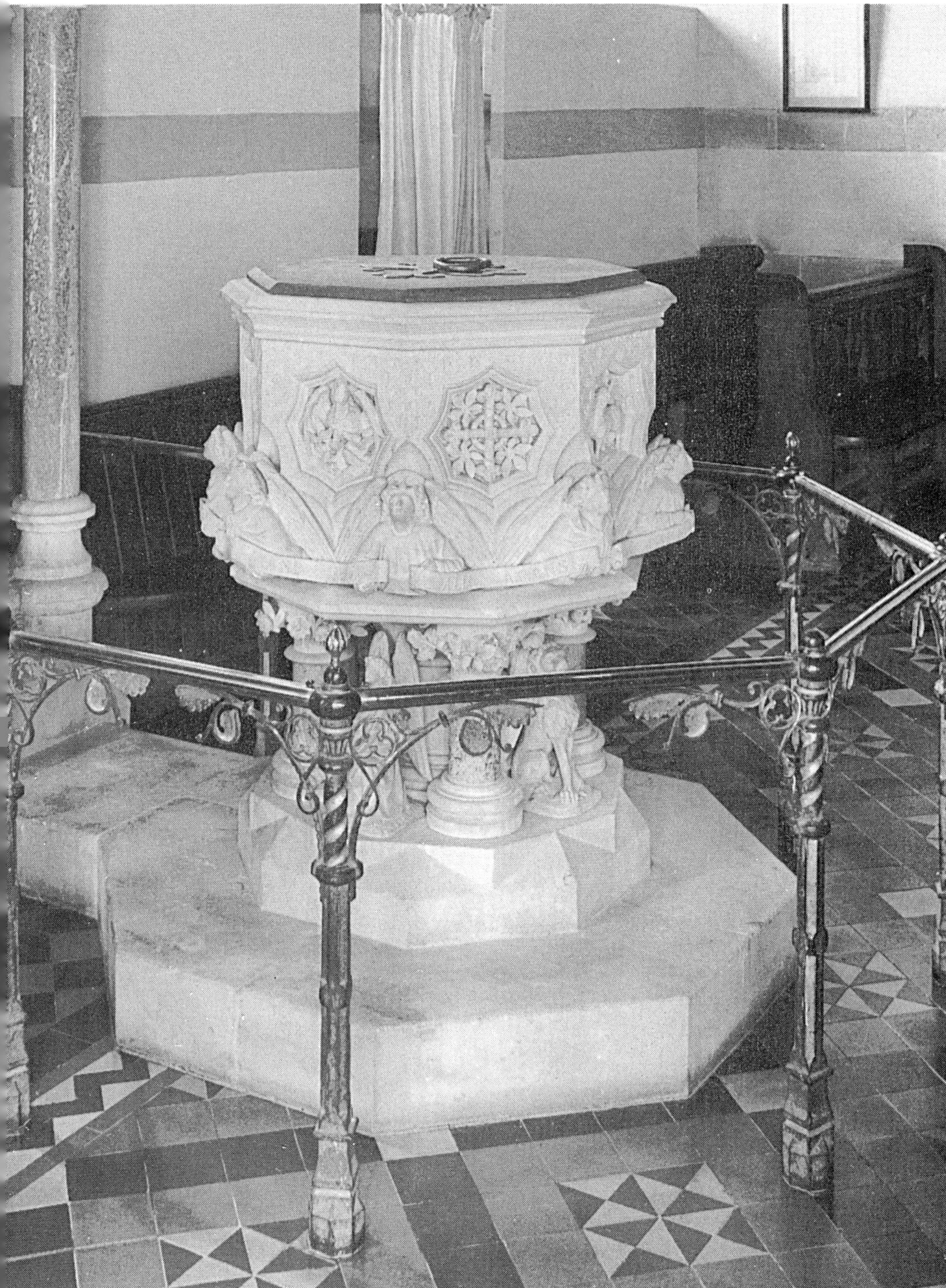

St John the Baptist, Huntley: font. (NMR)

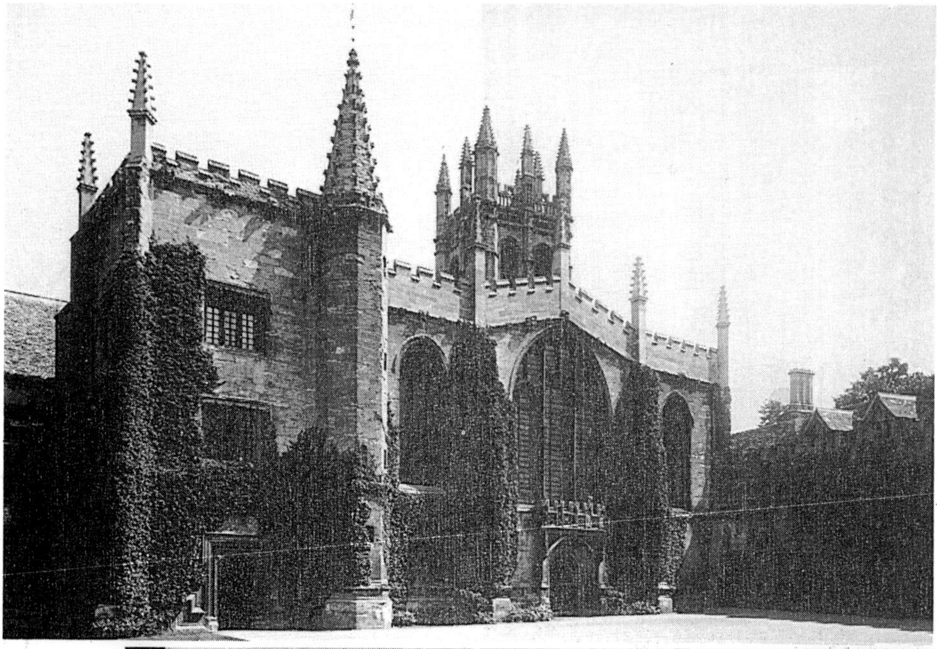

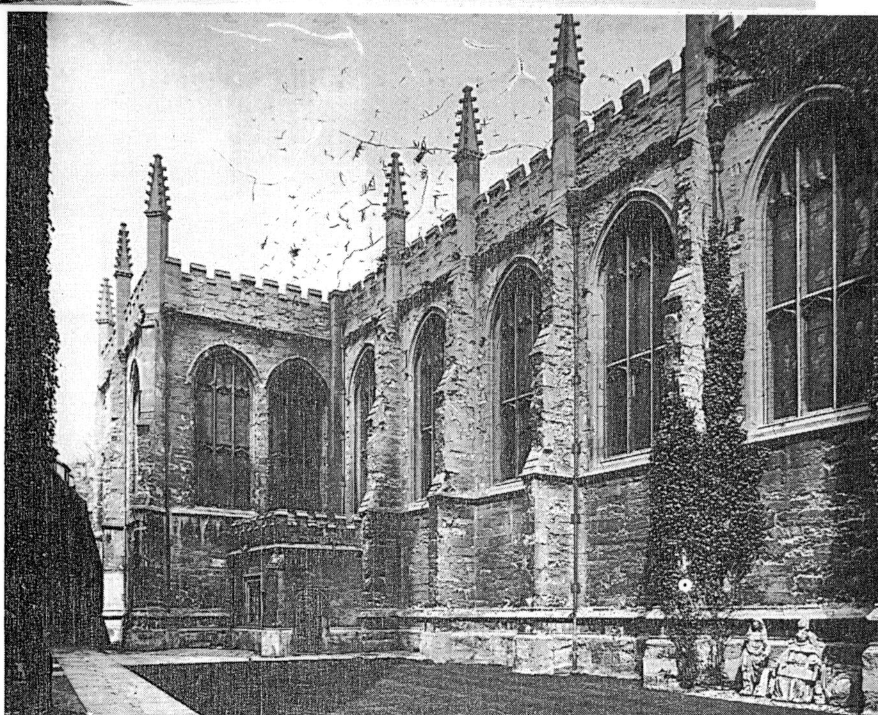

ABOVE: Magdalen College Chapel, Oxford. 19th century Oxford photographer Henry Taunt's view of the west end and BELOW: his view from the south-east. (Both NMR)

Men and Angels

In 1864 Thomas Earp produced no fewer than thirty-nine effigies of Old Testament characters to fill empty niches in the newly-restored altar screen of Magdalen College Chapel, Oxford. These restorations had been undertaken earlier by Cottingham between 1829 and 1834, developing some earlier work by Wyatt. The new work included new stalls, and a stone reredos, extending the full height and breadth of the east wall.

Religious scruples of the time had prevented the filling of the thirty-nine niches. The historic theological controversies associated with the Oxford Movement were still continuing. Newman's conversion had caused a shock still felt. However, by 1864, as far as the divines of Magdalen were concerned, these doubts had been sufficiently resolved to allow the installation of the statues.

At the apex a tableau in bas-relief represents the encounter of Mary Magdalen with Christ after the Resurrection.

The completed scheme compares well with the reredos in Oxford's All Souls Chapel, restored by Scott with Geflowski's carved figures, or James Sherwood Westmacott's reredos in Newcastle Cathedral.

This was not the only occasion where Earp's work was affected by ecclesiastical disputes. In Torquay, Devon, according to Paul Joyce, the authority on Street, a reredos that Earp provided for Street's church of St John the Apostle in the 1860s underwent some tiresome adaptations before it was finally installed. The original design was of the Crucifixion, the figures consisting of Christ, flanked by St John, Mary and two other scriptural characters. For some obscure theological reason, this upset the Bishop of Exeter, the ordinary of the diocese. To his way of thinking, the whole design was 'papistical'. The Crucifixion was being presented as an object of worship, a concept unacceptable to worshippers of the Bishop's school.

Street was obviously disappointed and expressed great reluctance to accede to the Bishop's request to scrap the work, which was of considerable merit and the result of much labour. After a great deal of discussion and heart-searching, and chronic examinations of conscience, a compromise was agreed. Thomas Earp was instructed by Street to change the stylised representation of the Crucifixion, offered as a focus for devotion and relative honour or worship, into a pictorial representation of the 'Crucifixion scene', introducing an element of realism by adding on either side of the Saviour the two thieves mentioned in the Gospels, each on his own gibbet.

In this manner, it was thought, no one would be misled into offering divine worship to an image of Christ and the other accompanying saints if, among the group, were the two thieves who could not by any stretch of the imagination be held up as models of sanctity. No one came forward to complicate matters by pointing out that, according to St Luke, one thief at least was promised Paradise even as he was dying. In this way the objectors were satisfied that the reredos would not become an object for 'idolatry'.

The reredos was then put up and duly consecrated but, years later, when such theological scruples were seen to be of less significance, the thieves were removed, and the reredos was restored to its original, more pleasing and less cluttered design.

For the church of St Michael, Mark Street, Finsbury (London) Thomas Earp prepared a reredos intended as a memorial to each of the recently-deceased daughters of Rev Thomas Evans, vicar of the parish, and Mr Robert Brett. The reredos was executed to the designs of James Brooks FRIBA, the church's architect. It was made in Caen stone. It consisted of three panels, of which the centre representated the Crucifixion, and the other two the Virgin Mary and the Apostle St John. The backgrounds were in gilded glass mosaic.

Before Dr Tait, then Bishop of London, came to perform the consecration in 1862, he insisted that the vicar and the architect sign a declaration that the reredos be removed, if it was pronounced to be illegal by Sir Travers Twiss, the diocesan adviser. To quote a footnote on page xi in Volume I of St Paul's Ecclesiological Society's *Transactions*: 'The day after the consecration, Mr. Robert Brett and the architect waited on Sir Travers Twiss with the drawings of the reredos and, after a careful examination, he decided that there was nothing illegal in the design, and the reredos was allowed to remain'.

We would give anything to know what Thomas Earp made of all this involvement with bishops, deacons, evangelists, crucifixions, angels, and similar other-worldly matters. Did it turn his mind towards things eternal, and the state of his immortal soul? Or was he put off by the everlasting bickerings and hair-splittings that accompanied the decision-making of his ecclesiastical patrons and their clients? We know nothing of his spiritual leanings, but he must have offered thanks for the High Church movement in the Church of England, and for the increased demand for Roman Catholic churches, following the immigrations of the Irish and conversions from Anglicanism.

In 1864 Thomas Earp was elected an ordinary member of the Ecclesiological Society, on Street's recommendations. The watchword of the Society was 'Truthfulness in construction and respect for the visual qualities of the material. Strength, utility, and reality constitute true beauty'.

Most of his commissions during this decade came from Street, and in 1863 the reredos he carved for Street's new church of All Saints, Brightwalton, Berkshire, was installed. Charles Eastlake remarked that the 'carved figures which enrich the altar exactly realise that combination of quaintness and grace which is so characteristic of medieval work'.

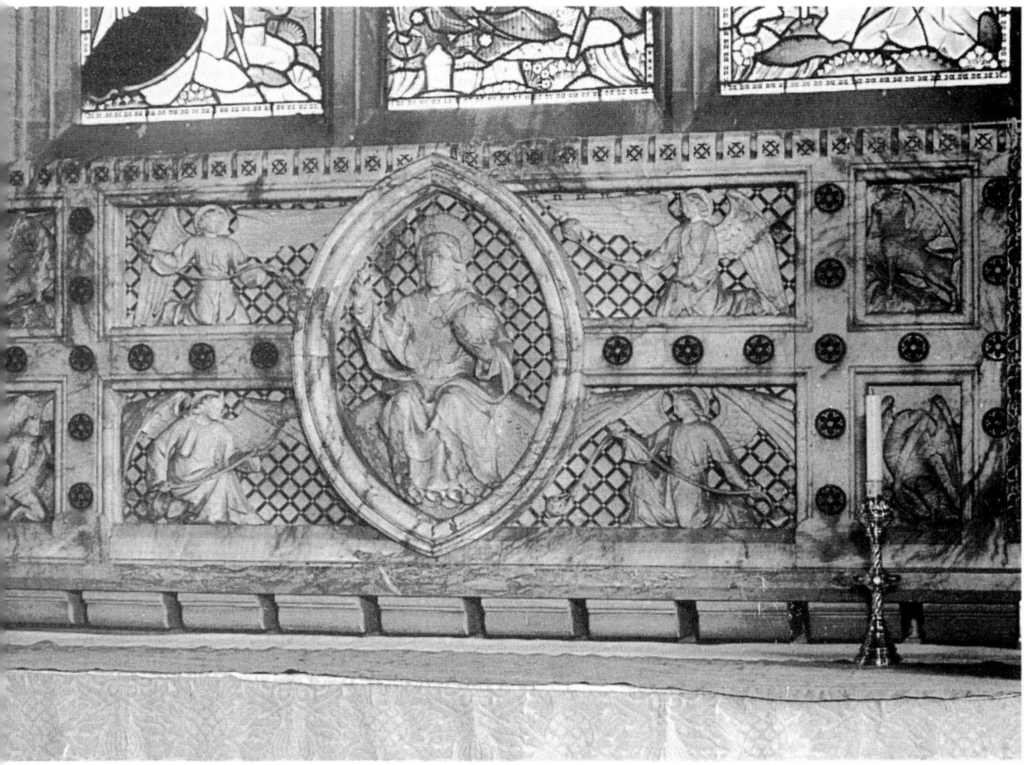

All Saints Church, Brightwalton, Berks: reredos. (NMR)

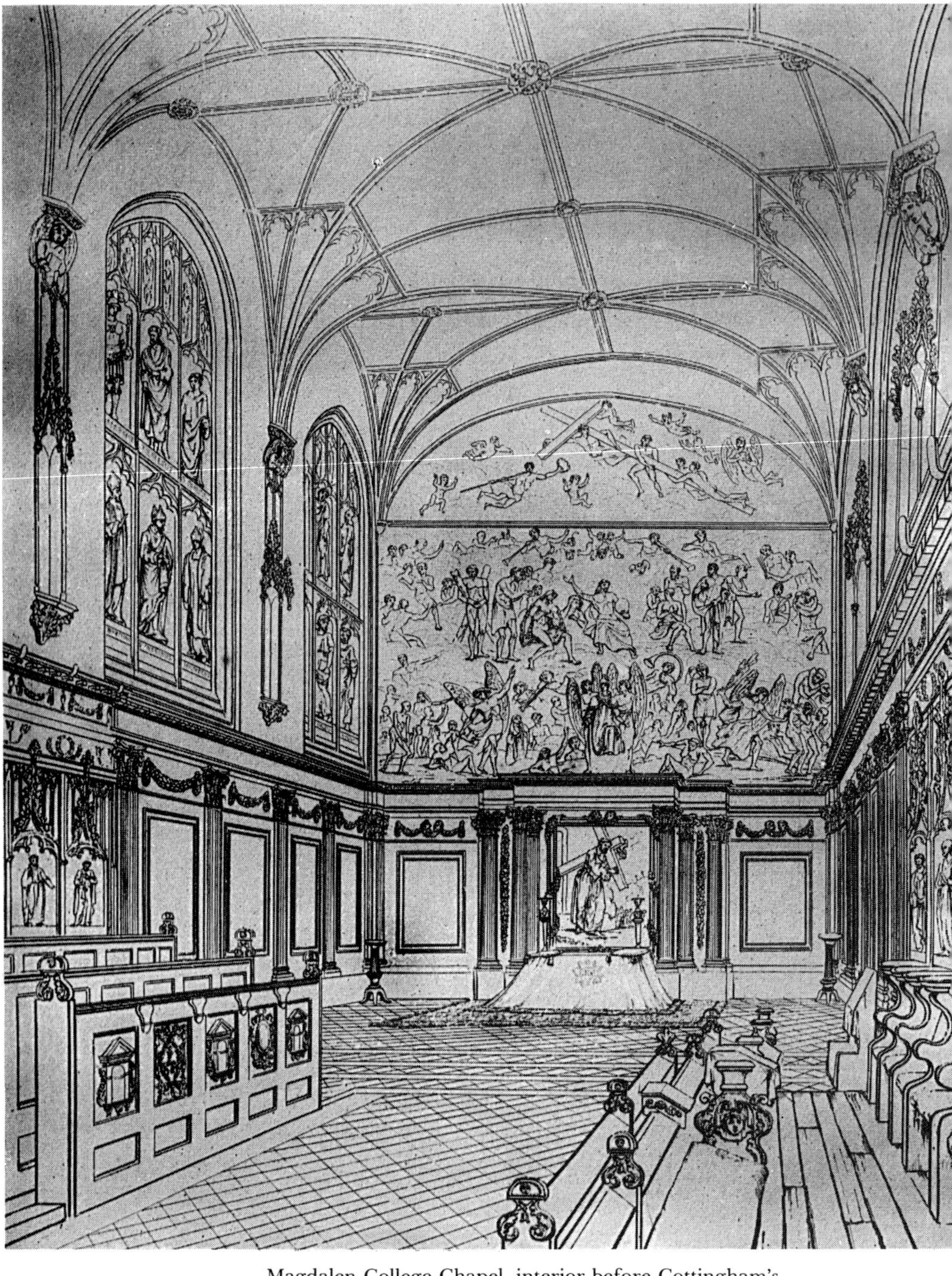

Magdalen College Chapel, interior before Cottingham's restoration. (NMR)

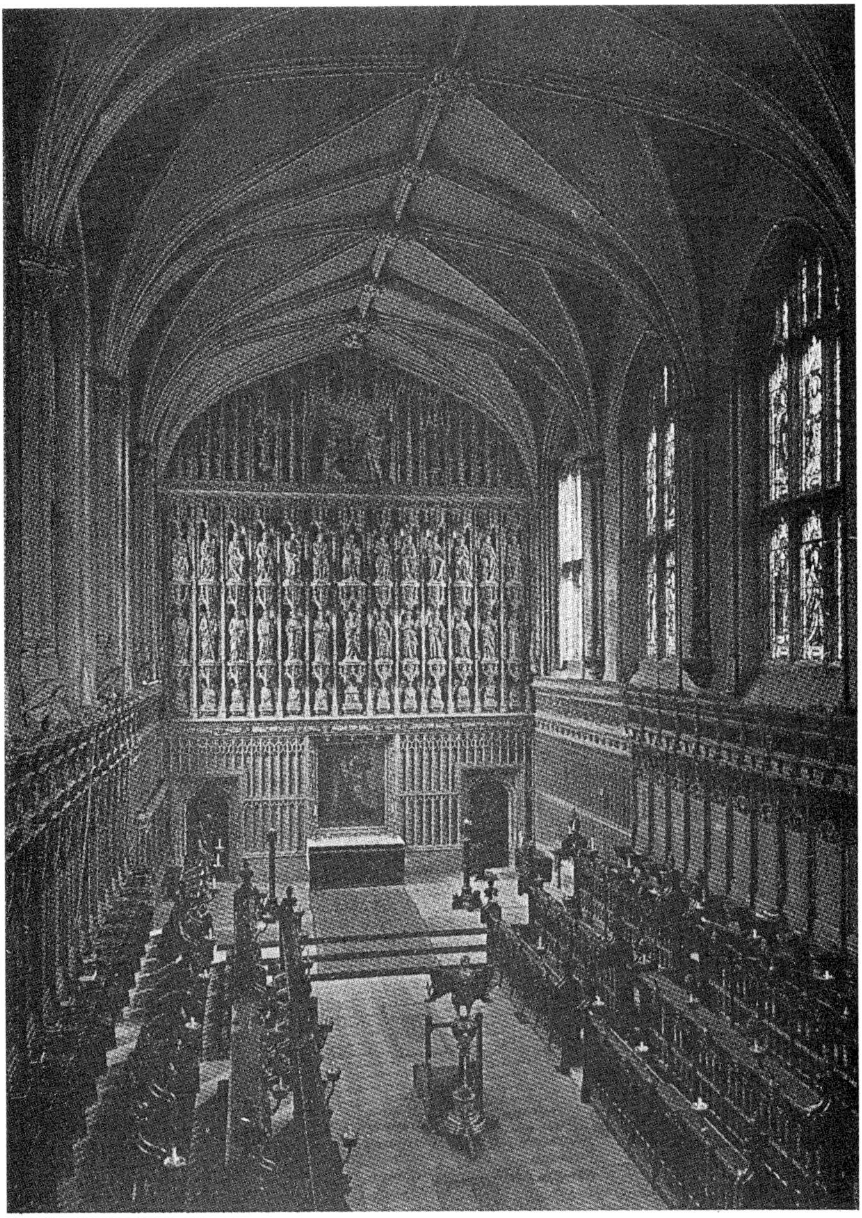

Magdalen College Chapel, as completed by 1865. (Oxford University Press)

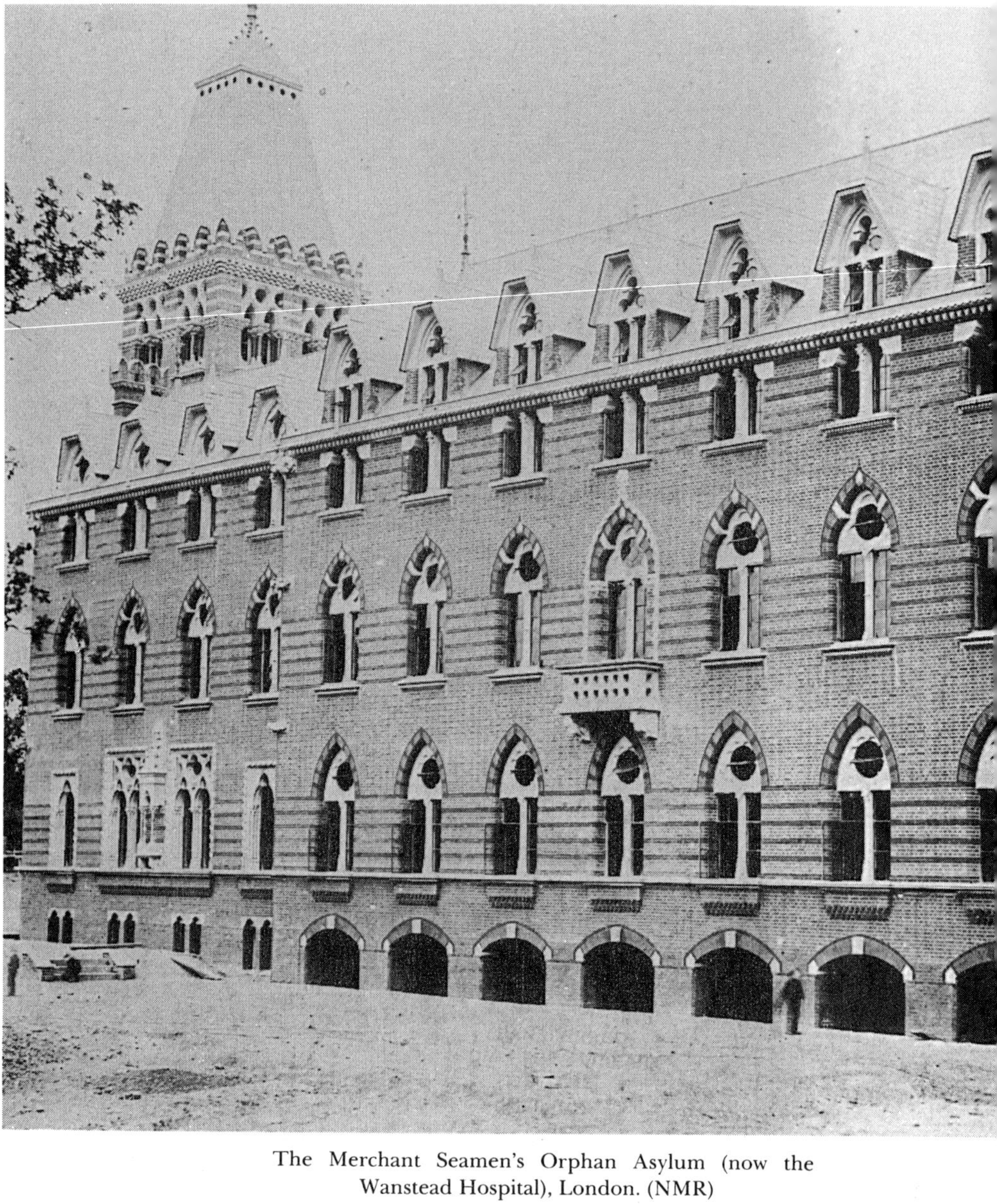

The Merchant Seamen's Orphan Asylum (now the Wanstead Hospital), London. (NMR)

Outstanding Achievements

In 1861 one of the last public duties of the Prince Consort before his death was to lay a foundation stone. It was for a new asylum for the orphans of merchant seamen on a site in Wanstead Forest.

Charles Somers Clarke, a former assistant to Sir Charles Barry, had been asked to design this building, for which seven acres of land in Wanstead had been purchased from Lord Mornington for just under £1,700. The building was described as 'A successful essay in the use of Venetian Gothic', and clearly Clarke studied Ruskin's *Stones of Venice*.

Thomas Earp was asked to execute the sculptural decoration: Clarke must have been well aware of his connection with the Barry firm. A maritime motif was chosen for the decoration and, throughout the building, the lintels and sills of the windows and the cornices are ornamented with representations of ship's ropes and rigging. Best of all is the carved relief of a shipwreck over the main doorway. Charles Eastlake called the decoration 'surprisingly rich for a utilitarian structure'.

Building progress was interrupted by an eleven-week strike of masons but, in spite of this, the work was finished in 1862 at a cost of £18,000.

At about the same time, E.M. Barry's scheme, commissioned by the South Eastern Railway Company, for the completion of Charing Cross Hotel, the station and its approaches, was nearing fulfilment. The station and hotel occupied the site of what was once called Hungerford Market. It completed the extension of the South Eastern Railway from London Bridge, and the heavy girder bridge that carried the lines across the Thames replaced Brunel's graceful suspension bridge, which was moved to Clifton. The piers that supported are still there, as part of the newer structure.

In the station forecourt, Barry executed the erection of a replica of the Eleanor Cross that had once stood not far from that spot. This was one of a series of crosses that marked the halting-places for the body of Queen Eleanor (wife of Edward I) when it was being taken to London for burial. The Eleanor Cross motif was repeatedly used for architectural design throughout the period. It was, for instance, the basis for Scott's Albert Memorial, and was described by him as 'the most moving of all consort memorials'.

The new cross was designed for Barry by Field, and the exterior carvings were carried out by Thomas Earp. It is a slender, tapering structure about 70 feet high, made of Portland and Mansfield stone and of Aberdeen granite. The carvings are in the decorated style of the 13th and 14th centuries. In the upper storey are eight crowned statues of Queen Eleanor, four of which represent her with the Royal insignia. There is a kneeling figure of an angel at the foot of each statue. The Royal Arms of England, Castile, Leon and Ponthieu are depicted on shields in the lower stage of the monument. The castle of Castile and the lion rampant of Leon figure prominently in the decoration. The work was completed in 1863 and cost between £1,700 and £1,800.

An enigmatic entry appears in a contemporary issue of the *Building News* under the heading 'On The New Cross at Charing':

'Dear to the shareholders, this cross
'Uplifts its head on high;
'Why stands it there? the critic asks
'And Echo answers "Why?" '

'Carissima croce! che falté la?
'Ne so, car, amico, en verita.'

Seventeen years later, Thomas Earp was to carve a statue of Queen Eleanor herself, making an exact replica of that which stood in Westminster Abbey. It was installed upon the tower of All Saints Church at Harby, in his own home county of Nottinghamshire. It was near Harby that Queen Eleanor died in 1290. The statue was the gift of a Mr Freeth.

In the meantime, Thomas Earp had carried out other work not far from his birthplace. He had received a commission from Teulon for the exterior decoration of Bestwood Lodge, a house built for the Duke of St Albans, a descendant of Charles II.

Teulon was regarded as one of the 'rogue' architects of the Victorian era. His style tended to be reckless and conformed to no recognised convention; he was bold and adventurous and a law unto himself. He has been described by Pevsner as 'ruthless and insensitive'. The house itself has had many unflattering descriptions, but Thomas Earp had, as usual, adaptably carried out in 1864 the designs set before him. Carvings of Robin Hood and his Merry Men appear above the entrance porch, and all the other decorative work throughout the building is his. It is with no reflection on his own skill that we quote some biased commentator making this somewhat gruesome remark: 'The entrance porch is unbelievably perverse, looking as though a surgeon has been at work'. The critic was probably referring to the flying buttresses flanking the entrance.

A few years before, Earp had provided a heavily-carved pulpit for Christ Church, Basford, also a Nottinghamshire village. The designer was T.C. Hine.

In 1866 Thomas Earp's wife Isabella died, in the sixteenth year of their married life.

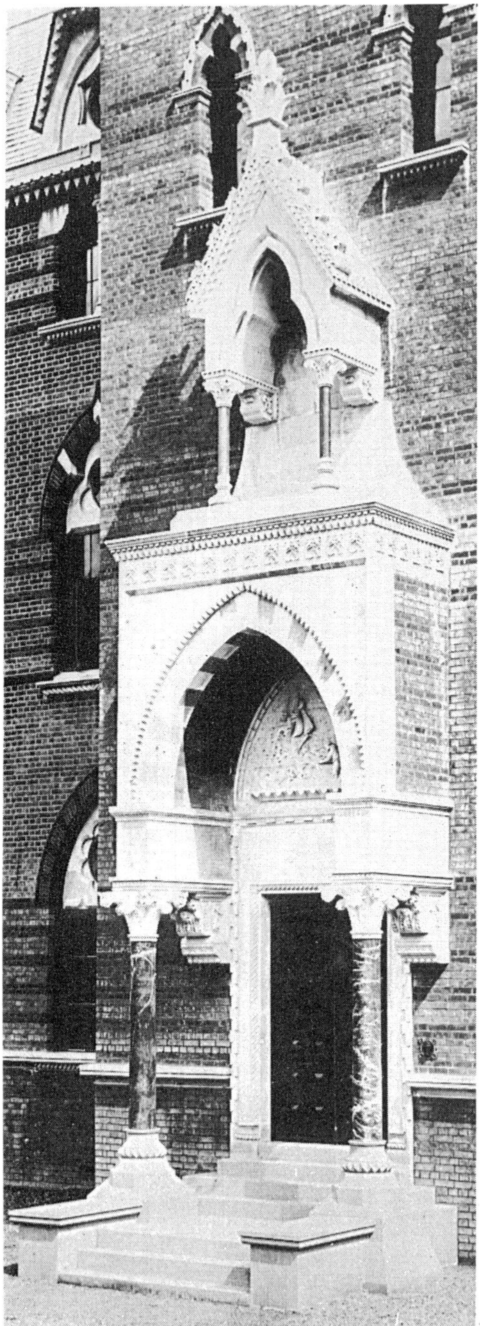

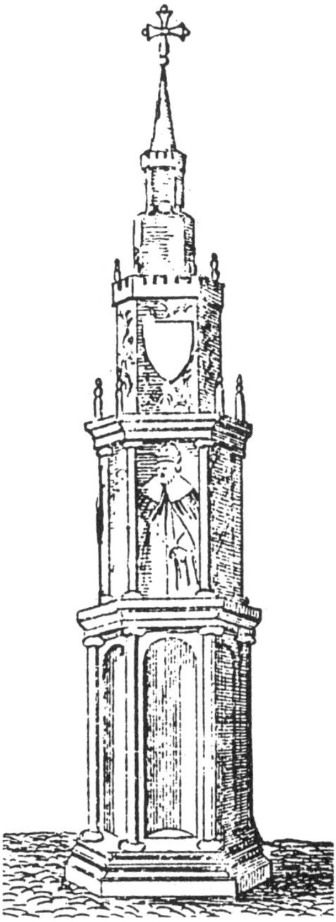

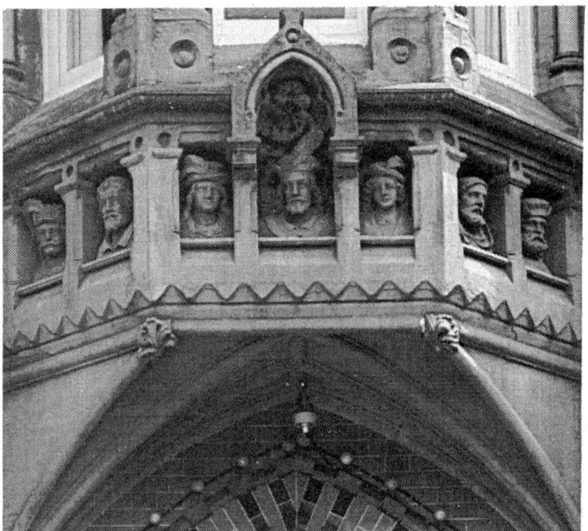

LEFT: The Merchant Seamen's Orphan Asylum (now the Wanstead Hospital). Entrance portico showing shipwreck scene. (NMR) BELOW: Bestwood Lodge, West Porch, showing Robin Hood and 'Merry Men' sculptures. (NMR) RIGHT: Old Charing Cross (now replaced by the present monument).

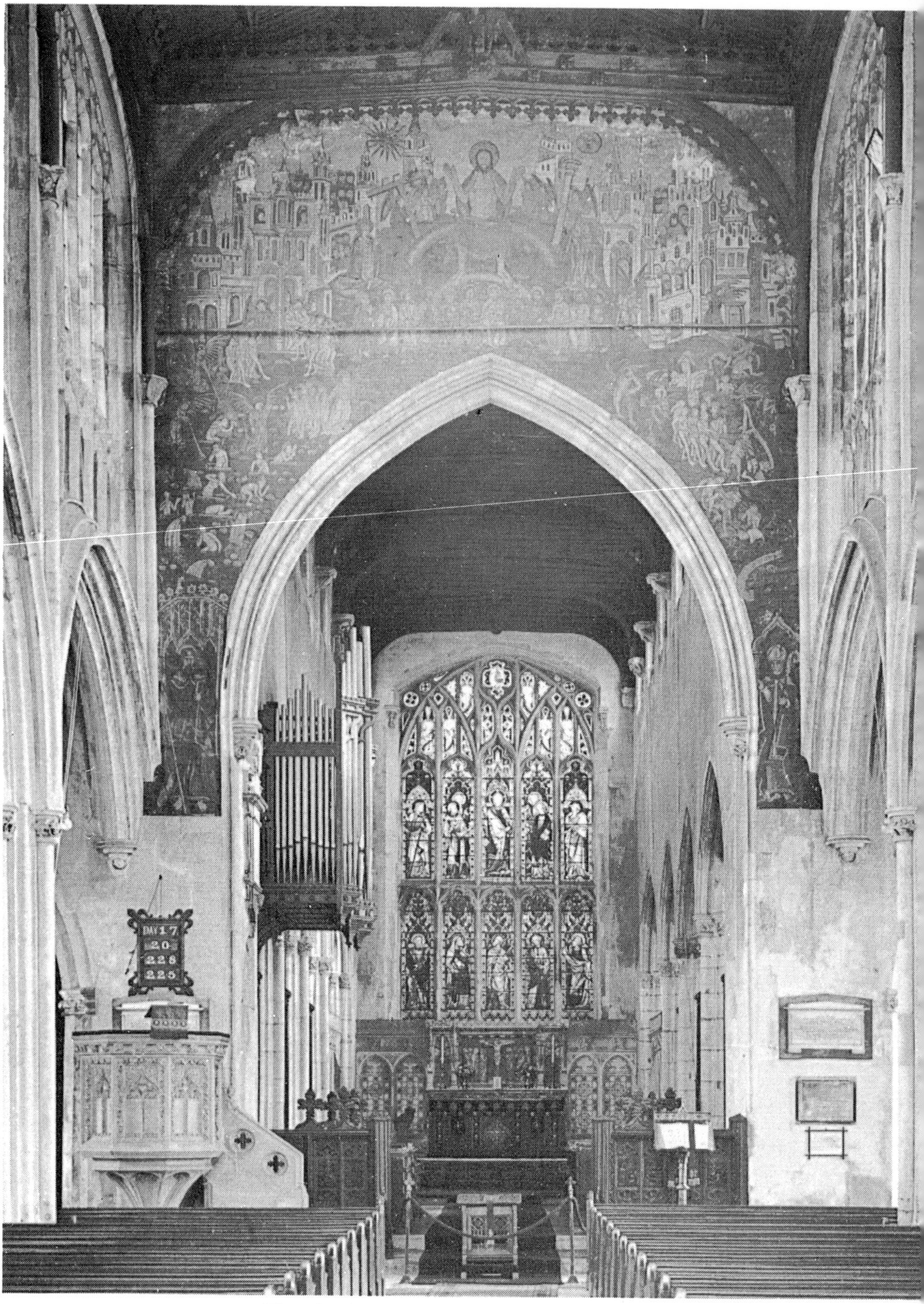

Church of St Thomas, Salisbury. the nave and chancel. The Street/Earp reredos can be clearly seen. Above the chancel arch is the famous 'Doom' painting. (NMR)

Memorials of Fame

Cholera was the great scourge in those days. South London suffered badly, which was not surprising, since both the Lambeth and Southwark water companies used water pumped direct from the Thames, already contaminated by sewers. In 1849 the *Illustrated London News* gloomily reported that 'Bells tolled continually while empty coffins were delivered like parcels on the heads of running men who knocked on the doors like postmen'.

Thomas Earp reached a watershed in his career on the death of his wife. Behind him were some twenty years of work – crowded, exciting, fulfilling and lucrative. He had nearly thirty years of active life ahead. It was the thirtieth year of Victoria's reign. William Booth had just founded the Salvation Army, Palmerston had died, and the Second Reform Bill was shortly to be passed. What effect did these events have on the life of the Lambeth sculptor and his family?

His elder daughter Isabella was now 15. Arthur, his son, was 12, and Edith Florence was eight. Two children had died in infancy. We do not know who looked after the children, or where they went to school. Their aunts-by-marriage, that is to say, the wives of Henry or Alexander, may have had some part in their care and upbringing. It is obvious that his business activities continued without interruption as, throughout the decade, many contracts were undertaken for Street, Barry, Blomfield and Teulon. Scott asked him to carve a monument to the Horton family to a design by Wilkinson, for erection in the churchyard of All Saints, Middleton Cheney, near Banbury. Another architect, St Aubyn, commissioned him to carve a new canopy for the restoration and much-mutilated monument to the family of De La Beche, in St Mary's Church, Aldsworth. For R.P. Pope, who rebuilt the church of St Peter and Paul at Luddesdown, Earp carved the reredos, designed by Ewan Christian.

In Portsmouth, Street was at work on the Royal Garrison Church, the fabric of which had been deteriorating for several years up to 1861. Formerly called 'Domus Dei' (God's House) it was founded by Peter de Ruupibus, Bishop of Winchester in 1212, as a hospice for pilgrims. It was surrendered to the Crown in 1540 at the Dissolution of religious houses. When Portsmouth became a naval base in the reign of Elizabeth I, a house for the Governor was built in front of the Domus Dei, which became the Royal Garrison Chapel. Although the Governor's house was demolished in 1826 the chapel was still used for parade services.

Ineffective attempts were made to repair the building from time to time but not until Street reported on the state of the building in 1861 was any work of restoration seriously started.

Thomas Earp carved forty-four oak stalls in the choir to Street's designs, all commemorating famous men such as Nelson, Wellington, Sir John Moore and Lord Raglan. During the Second World War the nave of the chapel was destroyed but the chancel was saved. Since then only the choir and the sanctuary have been preserved: the nave has been left roofless. It is scheduled as an ancient monument.

Street found much business for Thomas Earp at that time. Worth noting is the reredos that was part of Street's scheme for restorations for the chancel of the church of St Thomas à Becket in Salisbury in 1868. It is a marble tryptich, the centre panel of which encloses a crucifix, flanked by marble carvings of the traditional accompanying personages. It is a piece of work which affords a focus for the splendid chancel when viewed from the west end.

Thomas Earp was entrusted with the decoration of Street's new church of St Peter at Swinton, Lancashire, built to replace a chapel dating back to 1791. The chancel, chancel arches and piers were carved in naturalistic foliage. According to the book written by the vicar, Rev Leatherbarrow, Thomas Earp was paid £114 for this work, which was completed about 1870.

He also carved the stone ornamentation, including the reredos, for Street's church of St Mary Magdalene, Paddington. The reredos is a representation of the Crucifixion, with the twelve Apostles in a row beneath it, making a composition well-suited to the High Anglican atmosphere of the church and parish. The work undertaken at Street's church of St John the Divine, Vassal Road, Kennington, consisted of a pulpit and capitals, surmounting the tops of clustered shafts, supporting the tall arches of the nave. Little of this work remains, since the church was extensively damaged in the Second World War. Fortunately the church has been well restored and its spire is still a prominent landmark for South London. The pulpit was transferred to another church at Forest Hill after the War.

For Wimborne Minster, near Poole in Dorset, Thomas Earp executed a new pulpit in 1868 to replace a wooden Jacobean one. It is a bold object, contrasting somewhat with the mellow Norman stonework of the rest of the Minster. It was presented by Henry Gerard Sturt (later Lord Abington) of Crichel House. The former pulpit was transferred to Holt.

At Clifton, Bedfordshire, the extensive restorations carried out in All Saints Church by Mr Haycock of Shrewsbury included a reredos from Earp's workshops. It was of Caen stone, the centre consisting of a raised panel, carved in high relief, representing the Crucifixion with the Apostles Peter and Paul on either side, the whole surmounted by a canopy. Marble shafts are a feature of this work. It was donated by Mrs Miles of Downfield, Herefordshire, the mother of the rector.

In York Minster Thomas Earp provided a mural tablet to the memory of Frederick Vyner, killed by Greek bandits on Maundy Thursday, 1870. At the bottom of the tablet these words are carved, from the last letter Vyner wrote: 'We trust to God we die bravely as Englishmen should do'.

Thomas Earp, for his part, continued to live bravely. He was still at Kennington Road, but the family that filled his house some years earlier was no longer there. He shared it with a housekeeper and a maidservant. His sister Emma had gone to live in Wandsworth, where she had set herself up in her own dressmaker's business, depending for her livelihood upon the patronage of ladies of the well-to-do classes of Victorian London.

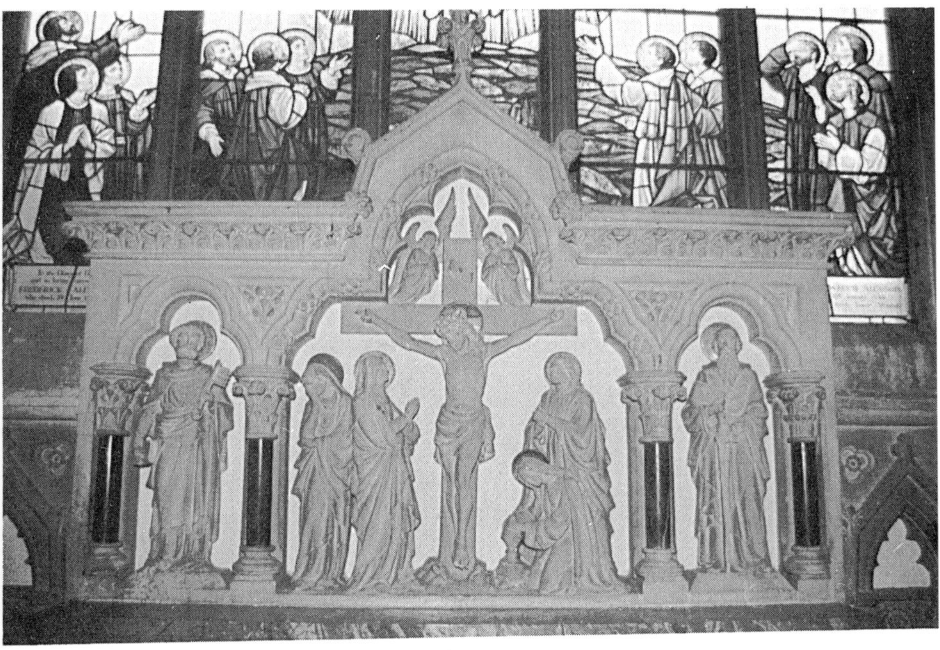

All Saints Church, Clifton, Bedfordshire: the reredos.

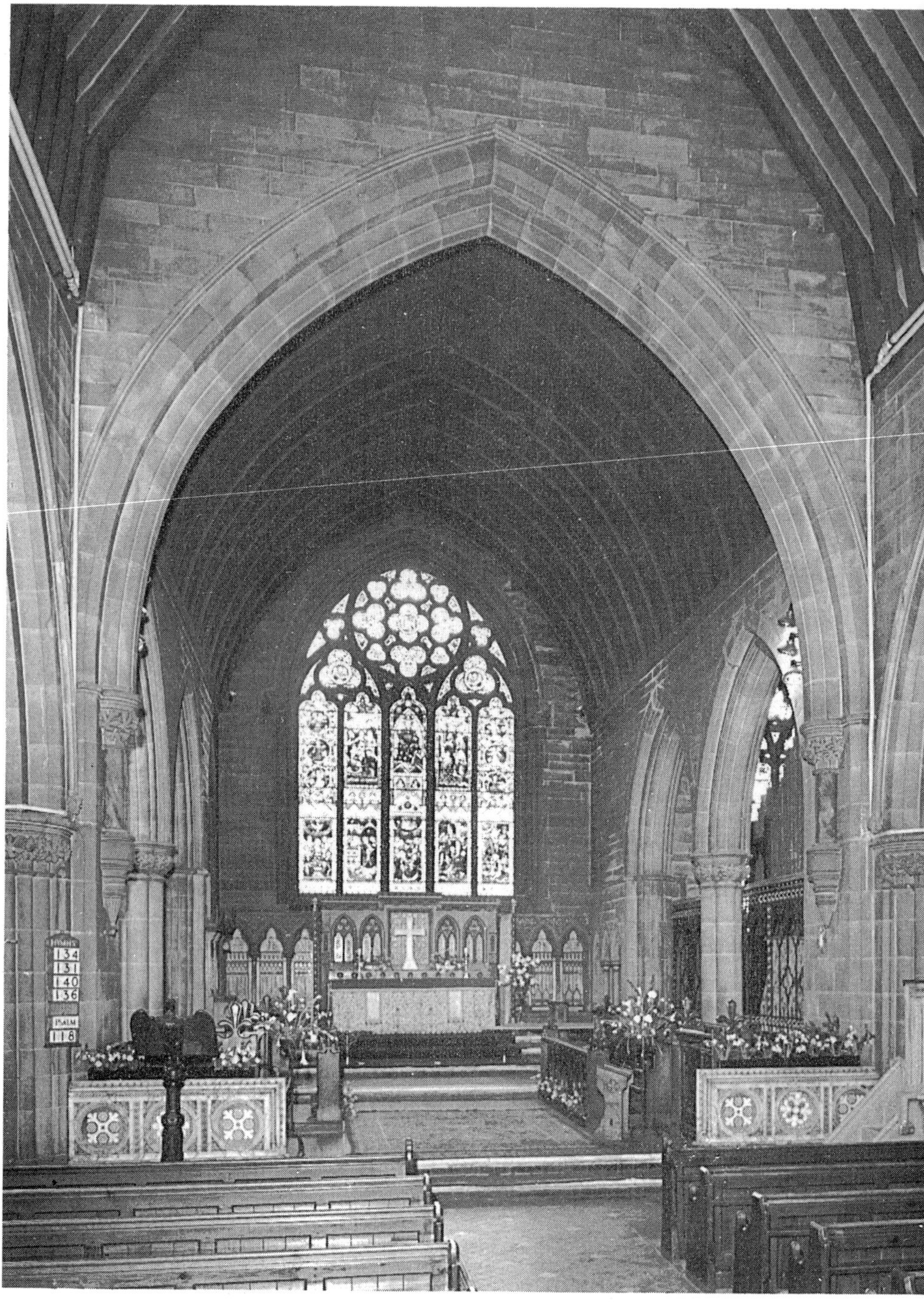

Church of St Peter, Swinton: Earp's carvings can be seen on the chancel arches and piers. (NMR)

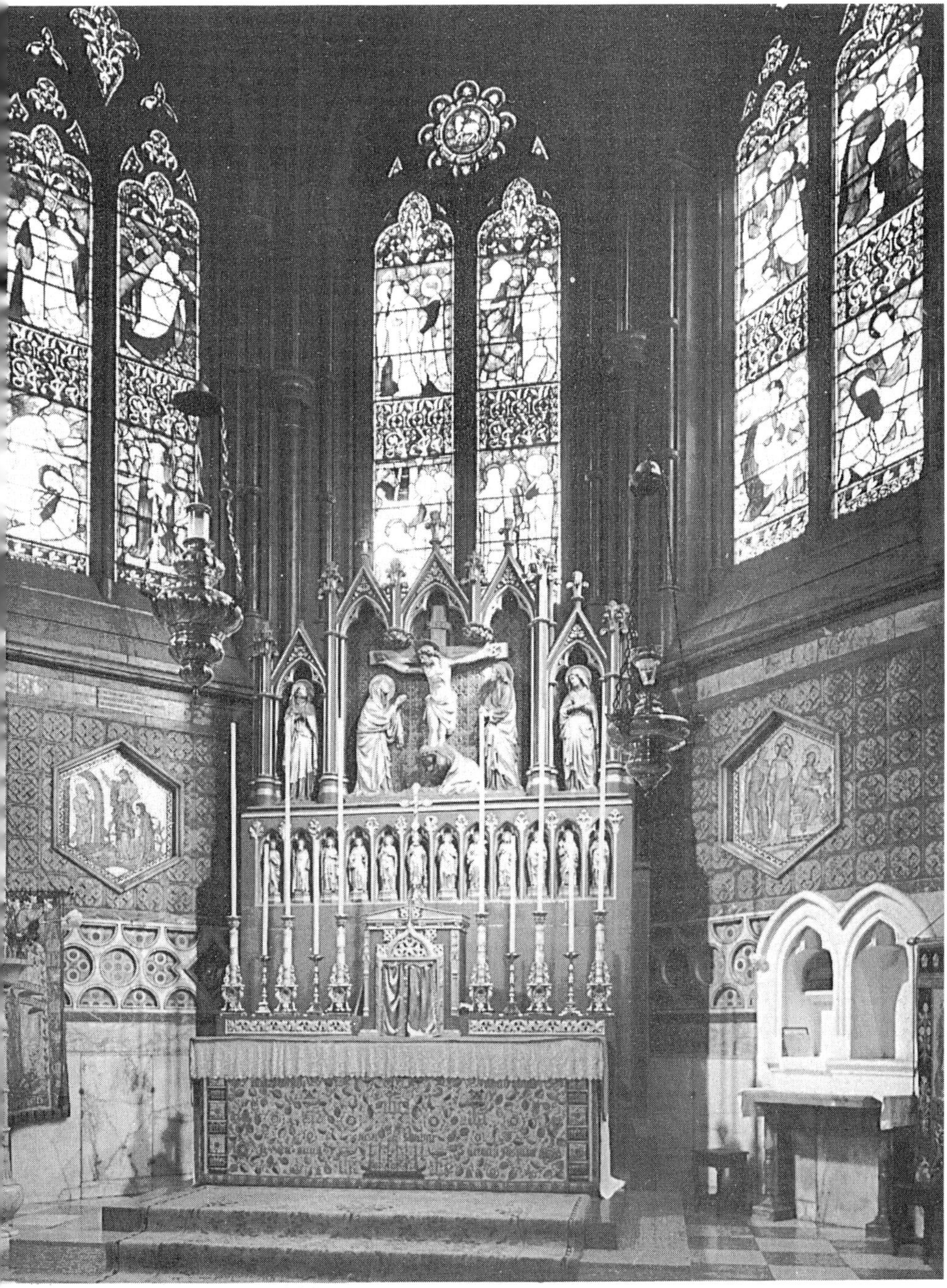

Church of St Mary Magdalene, Paddington, London: the High Altar and reredos,with the twelve apostles below the Crucifixion tableau. (NMR)

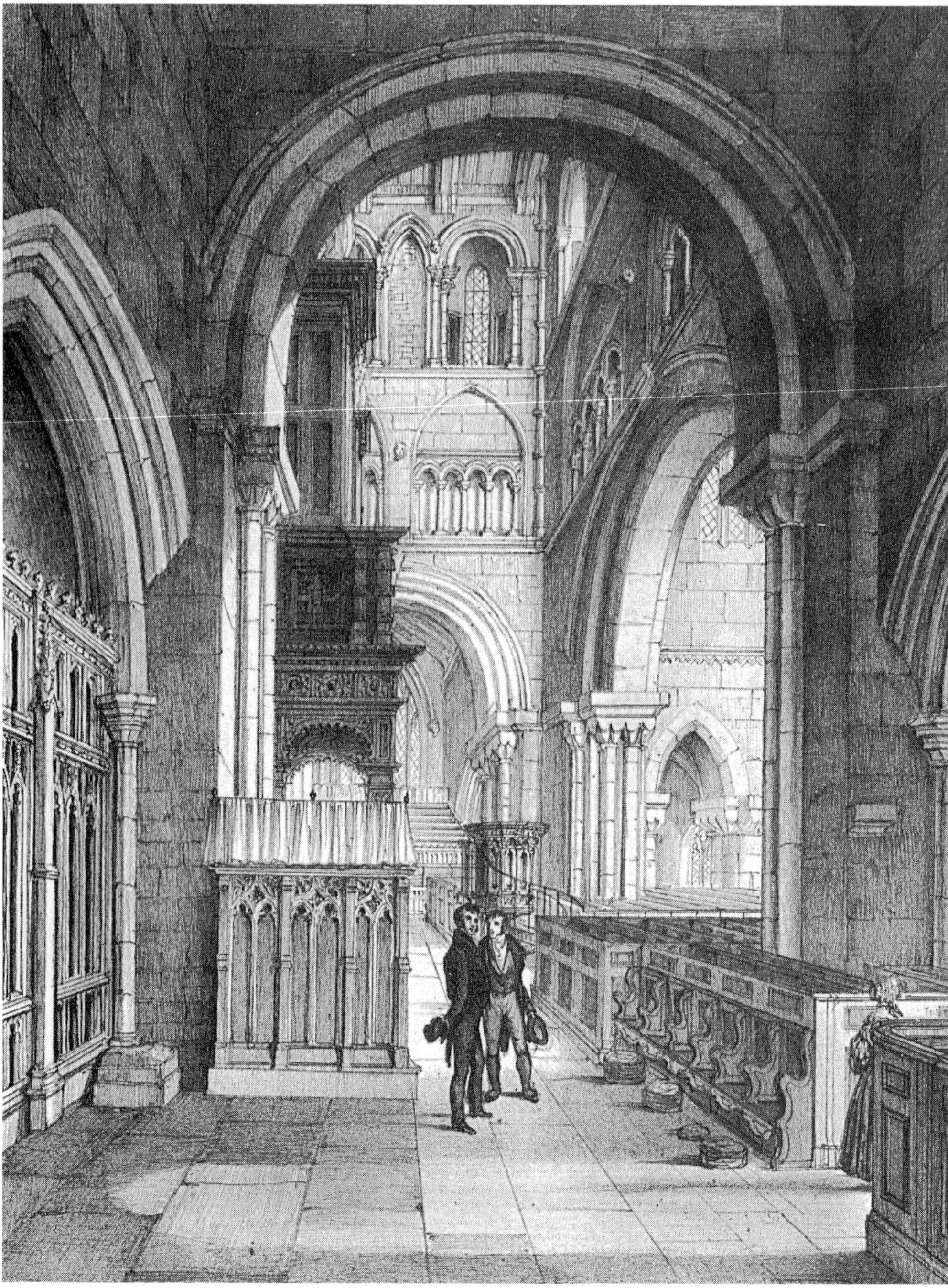

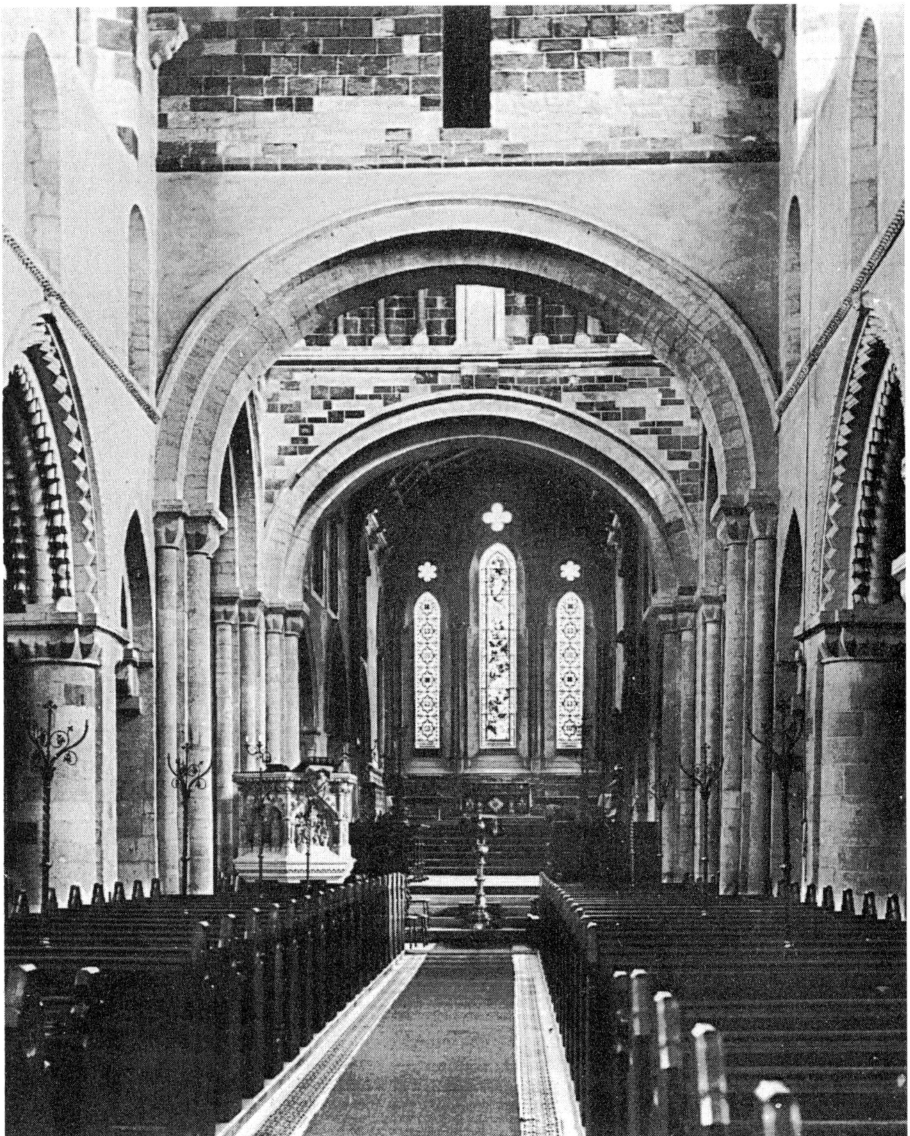

OPPOSITE: Wimborne Minster (Church of St Cuthberga). A print showing the former pulpit that was replaced by ABOVE: Earp's pulpit. (Both NMR).

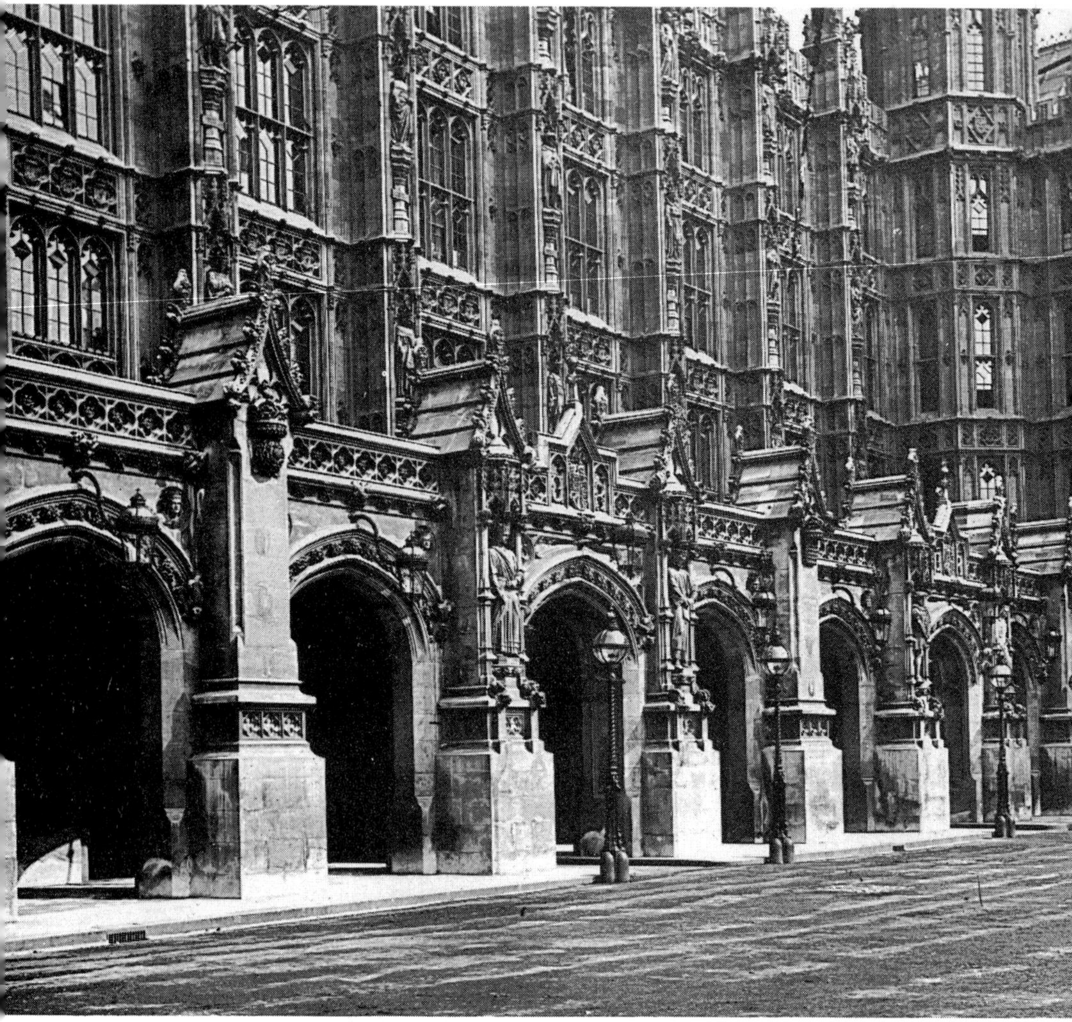

Palace of Westminster, New Palace Yard: cloister arches.
(NMR)

For Church and State

Sir Charles Barry died in 1860, his life-work at the Houses of Parliament still incomplete, and his son Edward had taken over. The House of Lords was completed in 1847 and the famous Big Ben clocktower in 1858; at Barry's death a flag flew at half-mast on the newly-completed Victoria Tower.

The building as a whole has had its critics. Pugin himself, although a co-architect with Sir Charles as far as the details were concerned, is said to have disliked the result. In later years H.G. Wells rather bleakly called it 'the illegitimate offspring of a Gothic Cathedral by a Flemish Town-Hall'. Nevertheless it remains London's most famous and exciting profile, and no one would have it any different.

It was the task of Edward Middleton Barry to bring the whole scheme to completion by designing the arcade and the enclosure to the New Palace Yard, at the north-western end of the complex at the foot of Westminster Bridge. It is not surprising that he called on Thomas Earp to carry out the decorative carvings on the cloister arches spanning the east side of the yard. His workshops were less than half a mile away, on the other side of the river, among the cluster of all the other stonecraft and sculpture firms that had sprung into existence as a result of this one project.

There is no direct evidence of Earp having done any earlier attributable work on the Palace of Westminster, in spite of his association with Pugin at Derby and elsewhere: George Myers had indeed failed to secure a major contract in the re-building. Pugin had completed the interior carving of the House of Lords by 1847, when young Thomas was nineteen years old: there is a possibility that he worked freelance, or as an apprentice, on some aspect.

The arches in the New Palace Yard are late medieval in style, integrated into the Gothic pattern of the whole. One arch at the north end and another in the centre have more elaborate ornamentation than the rest, offering access to the interior courts, and are flanked by canopied statuary.

In 1866 Samuel Sanders Teulon started work on St Stephen's, Rosslyn Hill, Hampstead. The founders had originally tried to appoint Ewan Christian, one of Teulon's closest friends, but he declined. Teulon was himself a resident of Hampstead and the site chosen for the church was not far from his home. He was descended from a family of Huguenots who had come to England in 1685, and he maintained their principles throughout his life. With his brother he was a director of the French Protestant Refugees' Hospital in Hackney, and his son became Vice-Principal of Chichester Theologicial College. He followed the Low Church or Evangelical line of worship in contrast to Street and his like, which appealed to large numbers of the wealthier patrons of the sort who disliked 'Popish' High Church tendencies and who had reservations about its preoccupation with the existence of slums.

Building started in January 1869 and the foundation stone was laid by Lord Ebury. That same year in December the building, or that part which was completed, was consecrated by Dr Tait, Bishop of London.

The church was completed by 1870, with the interior stone carving and decoration executed by Thomas Earp, consisting among other things of the nave capitals, full-length figures on the roof of the narthex and carved heads in the spandrels of the clerestory windows. On the exterior wall of the south transept the most noteworthy feature is Thomas Earp's group of King David amongst his courtiers, looking heavenward while playing the harp, during one of his more pious moments. John Ruskin, a devoted friend of one of the co-founders, Charles Woodd, considered St Stephen's to be 'the finest specimen of brick building in all the land'. Another contemporary comment was: 'An interior rich in decoration, that no good taste could ever take into insipidity'.

A different type of work to that required by Teulon's evangelical clients emerged for the Roman Catholics at Farm Street and at Maiden Lane, London.

Throughout the eighteenth century English Catholics had few chapels, often placed where they were unlikely to attract observation. At the time of the Catholic Emancipation Act of 1829 it was estimated there were only 60,000 Catholics in the whole country.

Two events affected the Catholic population. These were the conversions resulting from the Oxford Movement and the influx of throughout the country, especially in London and the industrial cities of the north, such as St Mary's of Derby and St Marie's of Sheffield. The church in Maiden Lane was one of the latest to be provided for the people of central London.

Land belonging to the Duke of Bedford had been leased by Father Cornelius Keens, and F.H. Pownall was appointed architect. Much difficulty arose from the poor quality of the ground on which the foundations were prepared, and the lack of light caused by the close proximity of other buildings. These and many other obstacles were overcome by Pownall's ingenuity: Bentley had had much the same problems with St Francis at Notting Hill.

A fine high altar in Caen stone was produced by Thomas Earp, providing an outstanding feature in an otherwise rather drab building. Monochrome figure and foliage work was picked out in gilt, producing an arresting appearance. In the church is other statuary, much of it movable and of no great merit. The church was dedicated to Corpus Christi, and was opened on 20 October 1874 with a solemn Mass at Earp's high altar, and a sermon preached by Archbishop Manning, himself a convert from the Oxford Movement.

A fire had destroyed a part of the church of the Immaculate Conception in Farm Street, Mayfair in London in 1865. This was the chapel of the Blessed Sacrament in the north-west corner of the church, which had been designed for the Jesuit Fathers by J.J. Scoles and opened in 1849. It adjoined Pugin's fine sanctuary and altar-piece, which fortunately escaped the blaze.

Henry Clutton (the architect of St Francis, Notting Hill) was commissioned to rebuild the chapel, which was afterwards designated the Chapel of the Sacred Heart, and an additional aisle was added to the east side of the nave to accommodate larger congregations. Thomas Earp carried out the decorative sculpture throughout the restored fabric. An account in the *Builder* for December 1866 describes the work, executed in Caen stone. The roof was groined, parallel ribs resting on a cornice supported by marble columns. The east end featured some French tracery, leaving some vacant spaces, which were filled in later years with a mural by the Rhineland painter, Herr Moliter. The walls of the chapel were lined with polished alabaster with inlaid designs.

Another place of Catholic worship where Thomas Earp contributed work was the Convent of the Assumption in Kensington. He was responsible for the decoration of the chapel and the high altar. However, today little or nothing remains of this work, due to war damage, and some over-zealous alteration to conform to liturgical changes.

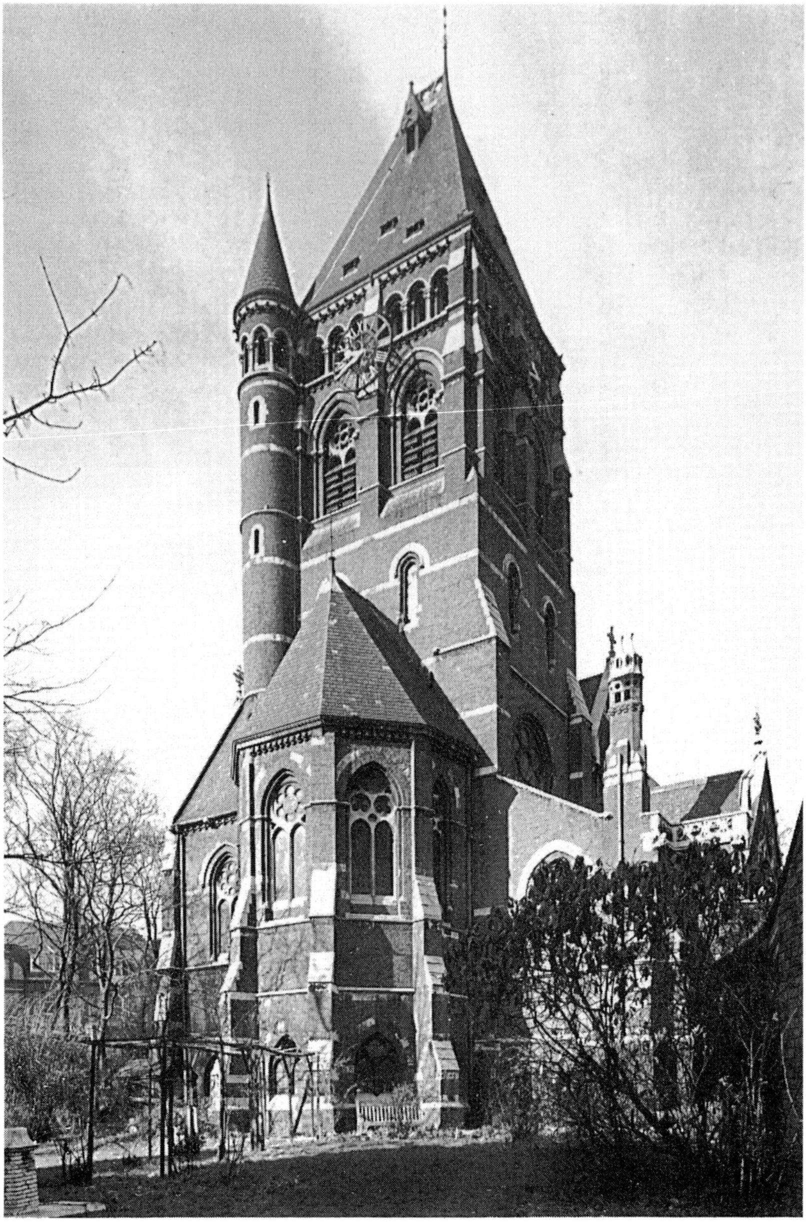

St Stephen's, Rosslyn Hill, Hampstead: view from north-east (NMR)

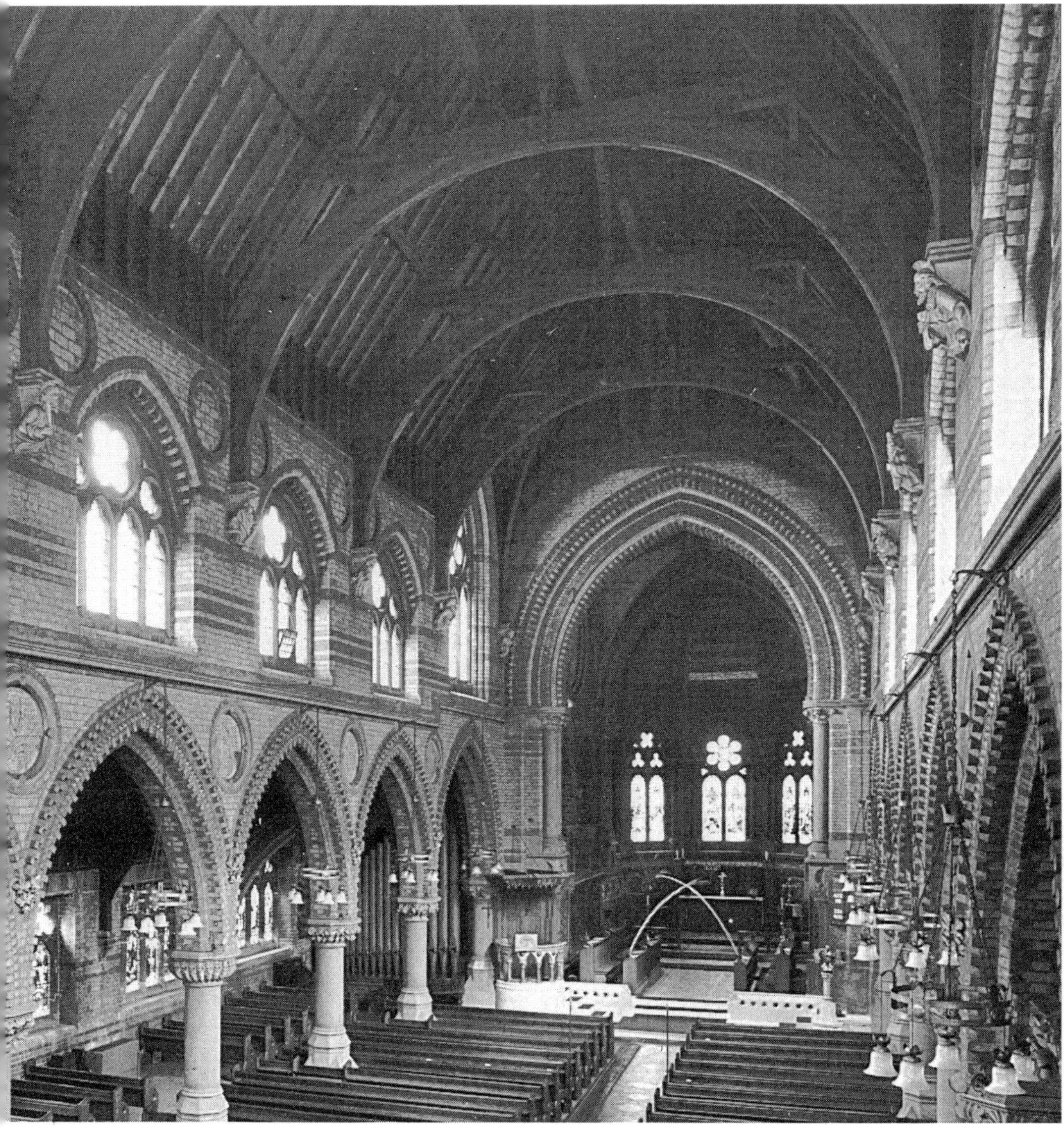

St Stephen's: the Nave. (NMR)

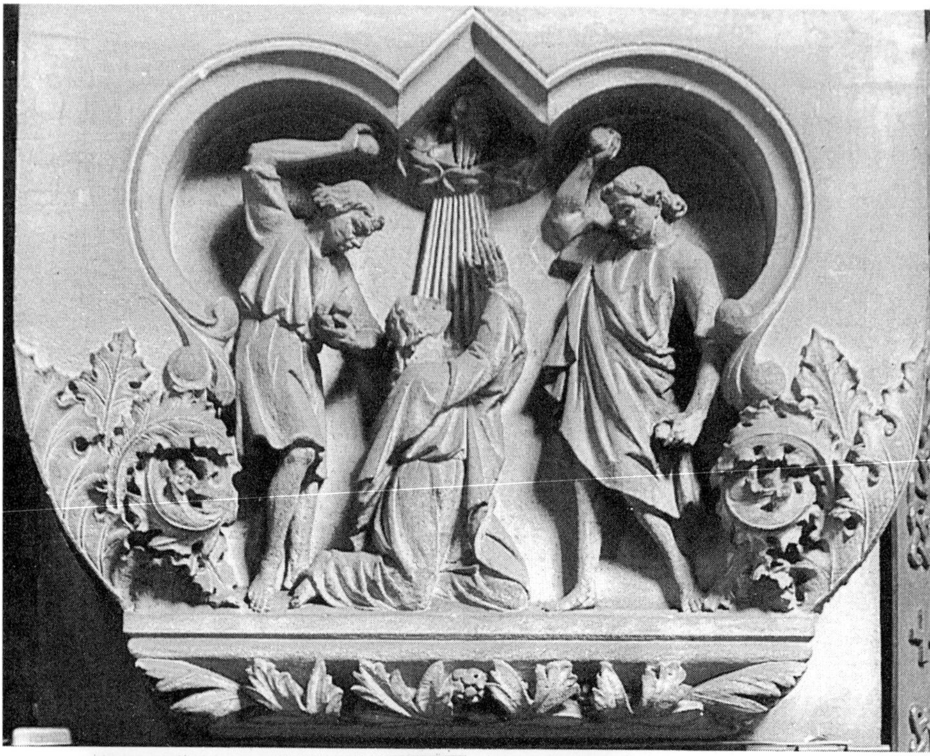

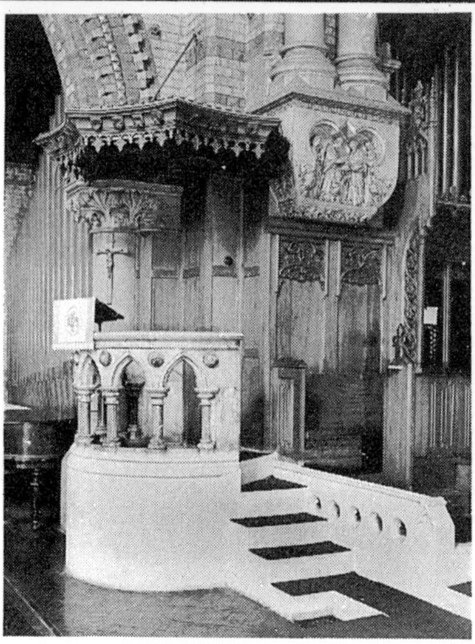

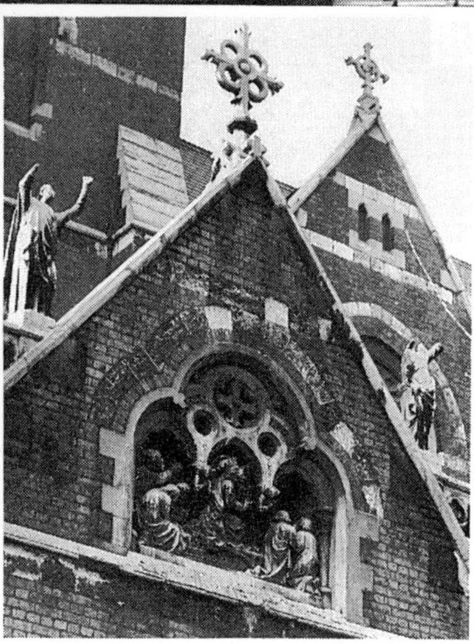

ABOVE: St Stephen's, Rosslyn Hill: corbel detail showing martyrdom of Stephen; LEFT: pulpit and RIGHT: King David group. (All NMR)

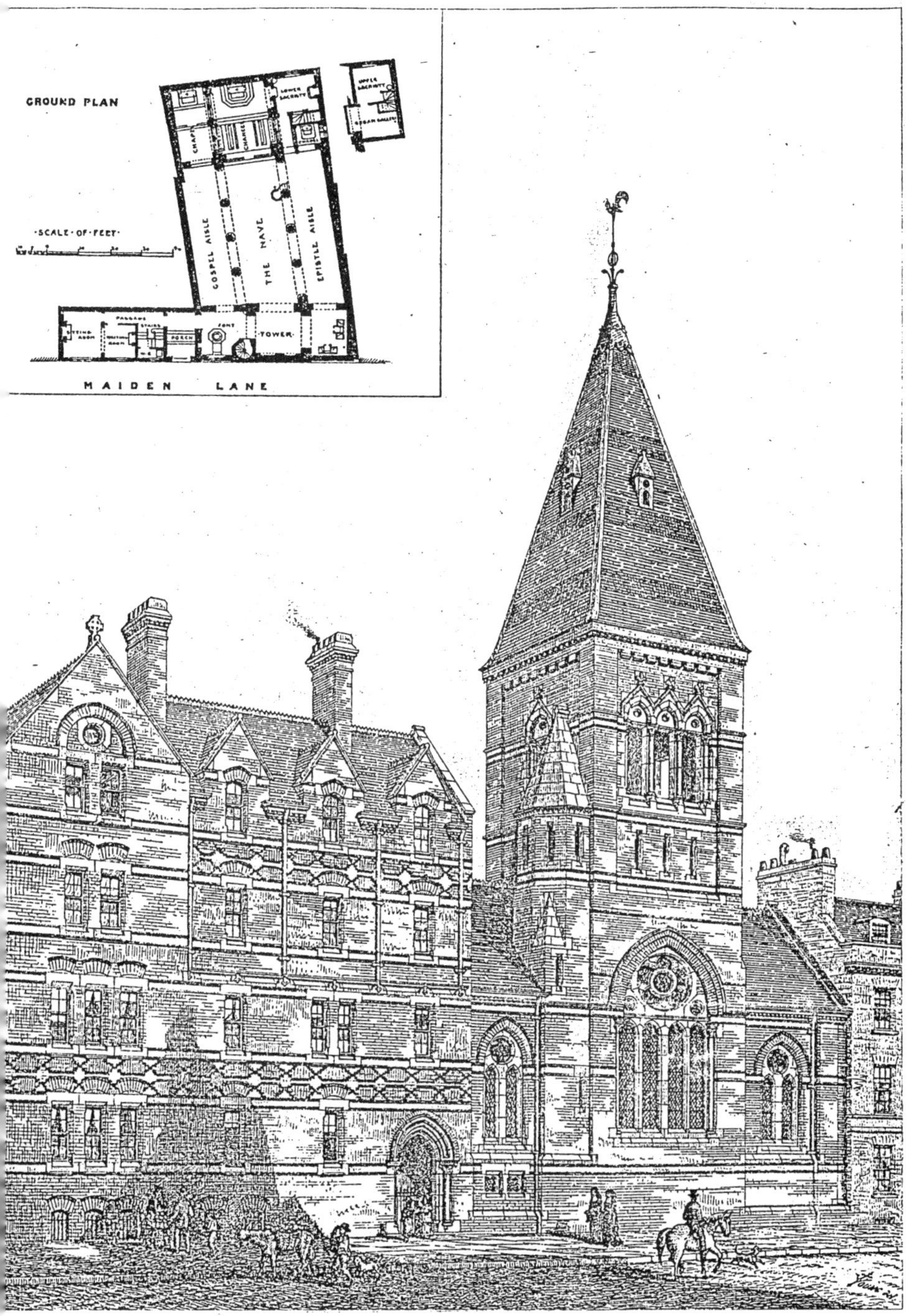

Corpus Christi, Maiden Lane, London. (BN)

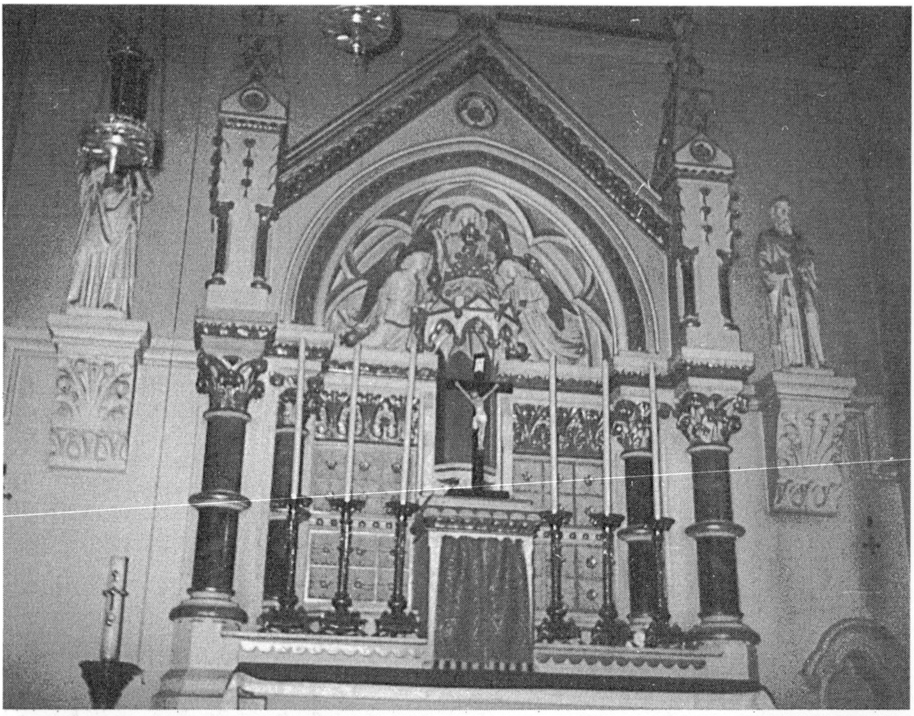

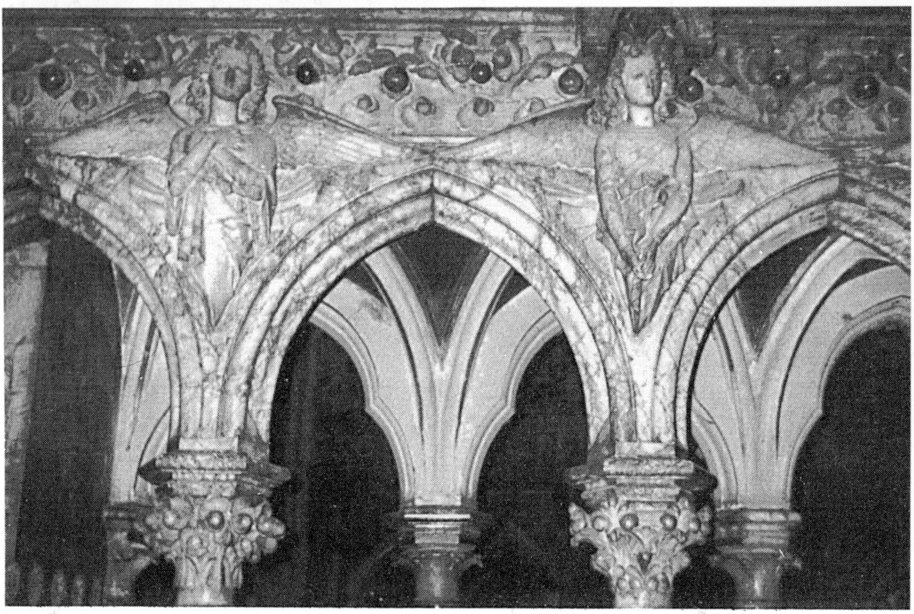

ABOVE: Corpus Christi, Maiden Lane: High Altar; BELOW: Jesuit Church, Farm Street, London: side chapel carving.

A Palace for Justice

Thomas Earp's main patron, George Edmund Street, continued calling on him to fulfill numerous commissions for the High Church of England, the 'Via Media'. The font provided by Earp for the baptistry of All Saints Church, Denstone, Staffordshire reflects the generosity of the patrons who endowed it. Designed by Street in the 1860s, it is in the form of four angels, forming a square composition. There is a unity in the work, their hands almost touching, their wings outstretched. In the same church is the Earp reredos with three arches, the centre enframing a Crucifixion and the outer ones unaccountably empty. There is also Earp's pulpit, a round structure in marble and alabaster, featuring two roundels with a cruciform motif on each side of a marble column, and an angel at the base.

By contrast the pulpit of SS Peter and Paul, Shiplake, Oxfordshire is to a plain design by Street, and the pointed arch motif carved by Thomas Earp is unadorned by figures, reflecting the desires of the worshippers. The reredos, too, is worked in a foliage pattern with only a small crucifix in the middle.

In Southampton, the church of St Mary was built by Street on the site of an older one in 1880 and the reredos Thomas Earp carved for the High Altar remains the only piece surviving today, after extensive damage in World War II. It now adorns the wall of the south transept, and consists of a Nativity scene.

Towards the end of the decade the long association between Earp and Street was drawing to its close. The work of designing and carrying out the building of the new Royal Courts of Justice had been given to Street, and it is proof of the high regard for Thomas Earp's reputation that the architect should turn to him for the execution of his designs for the decorative stonework.

Of the famous history of this building, and of the competition among architects to be awarded the designing of it, and of the clearance of the slums on the north side of the Strand to make room for it, enough has been written. All the stone carving inside and outside the Law Courts, including the statues of Christ, King Solomon, Moses and King Alfred the Great on the roof of the buildings, were carried out by Thomas Earp and his workmen, of whom H.T. Margetson was his foreman. A.E. Street, in the biography of his father, wrote: 'The carving throughout the Law Court is probably of as high a character as any Gothic carving which has been executed in our day, and does every credit to the men who were engaged on it'.

It was the last work Earp's firm did for Street. The strain had proved too much for the architect and, before its completion, he died of a stroke. His son carried on and saw the work through to its finish. When Queen Victoria opened the Law Courts on 6 December 1882, it was the only shadow over the occasion, expressed feelingly in an address presented by the workmen to the Queen: 'Our one regret is that the great master whose designs we have carried out should not have been spared to see this day'.

The Law Courts are in themselves an epitome of Street's architectural style and indeed his way of thinking, executed through the hands of Thomas Earp and Margetson. The design as a whole did not lend itself to over-elaborate decoration, but what stonecarving was carried out was done particularly to Street's own detailed supervision. The architect himself made the clay models, a task in which he became greatly absorbed and which gave him obvious enjoyment. The Office of Works gave him a free hand as to whom he employed and the terms of payment.

Of the four law-givers whose statues stand on the roof, Moses alone faces north, looking down on Carey Street. Christ, King Solomon and King Alfred face the Strand, exemplifying the Christian and liberal basis of English Common Law and the interpretation of traditional law. Of all the other carvings on the building's exterior shields bearing the coats of arms of notable contemporary jurists are worthy of remark. Much else was conventional foliage, but a humorous comment on legalistic squabbling is afforded by figures of cats and dogs adorning the judges' entrances on the north side.

How much litigation took place within this place of justice, involving the affairs of sculptors and their patrons and clients as a result of business contracts completed or incompleted, including the affairs of Thomas Earp himself after his death, is anybody's guess.

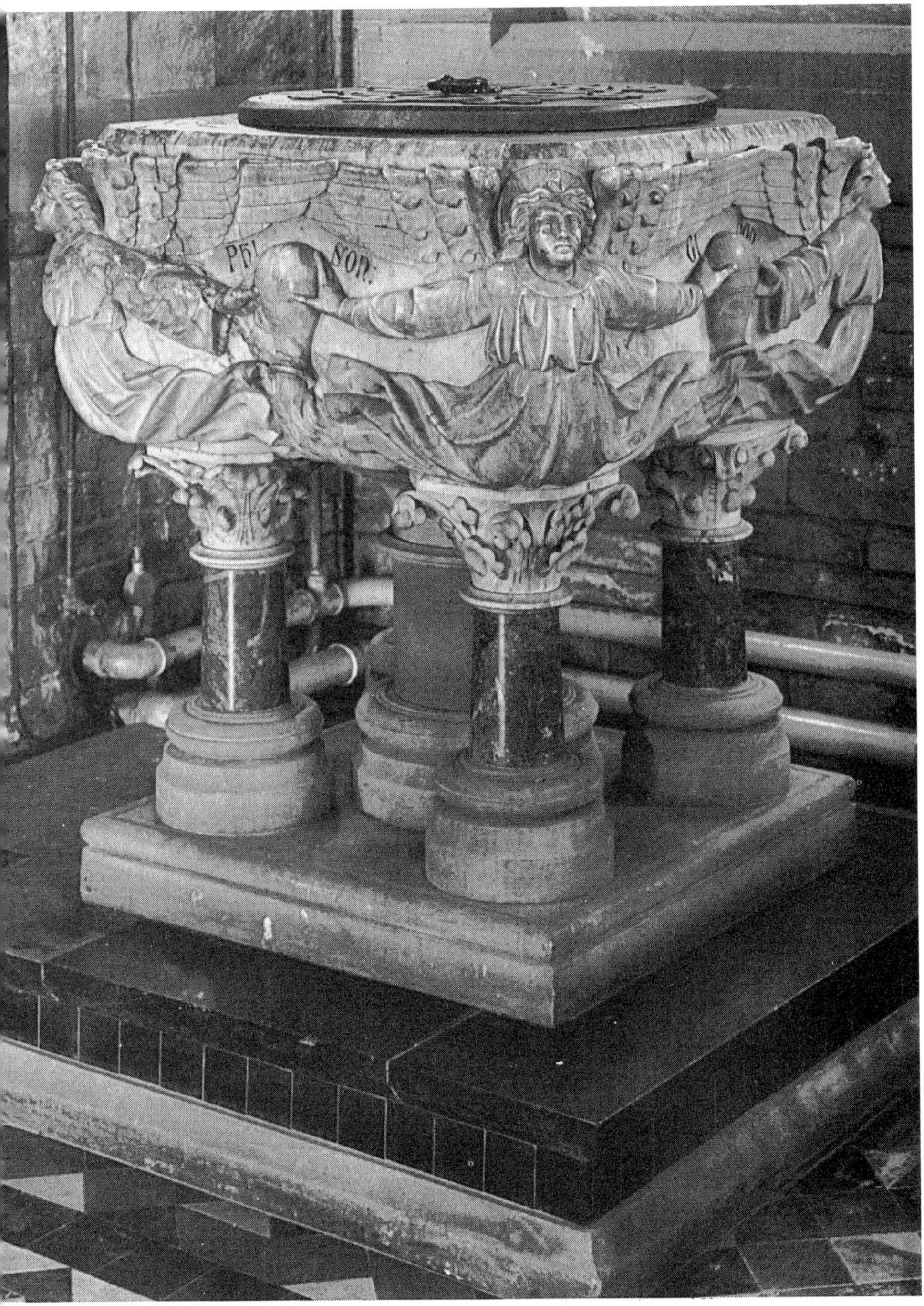

All Saints Church, Denstone, Staffs: font. (NMR)

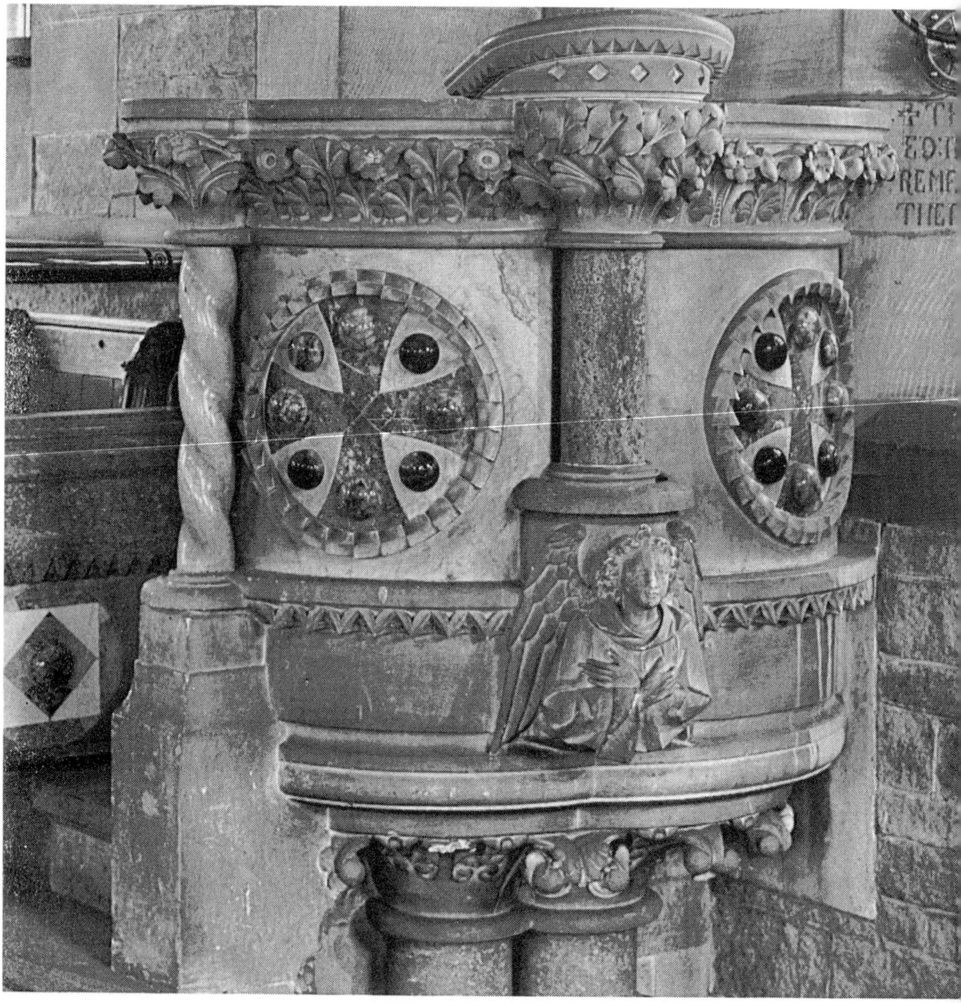

All Saints Church, Denstone, Staffs: pulpit. (NMR)

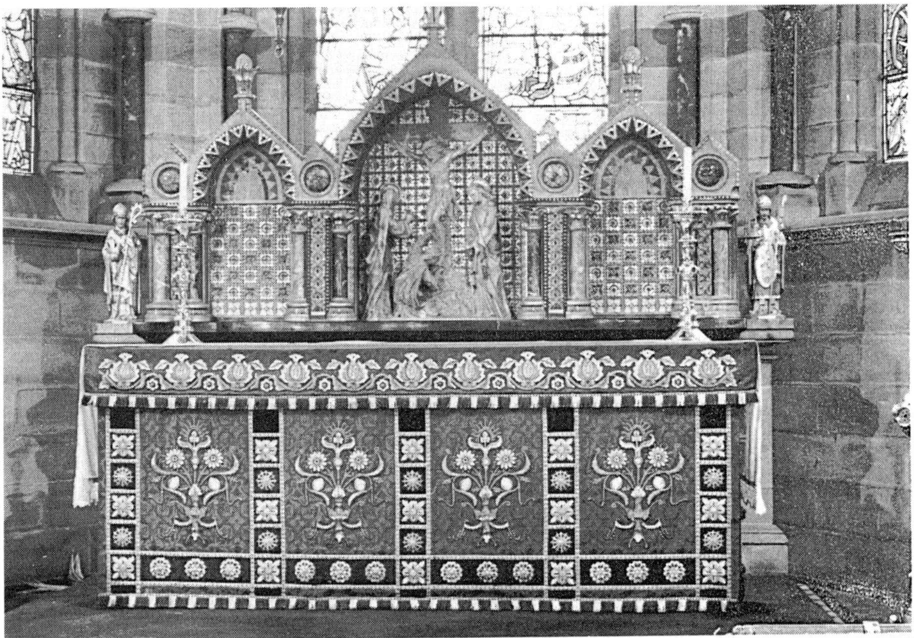

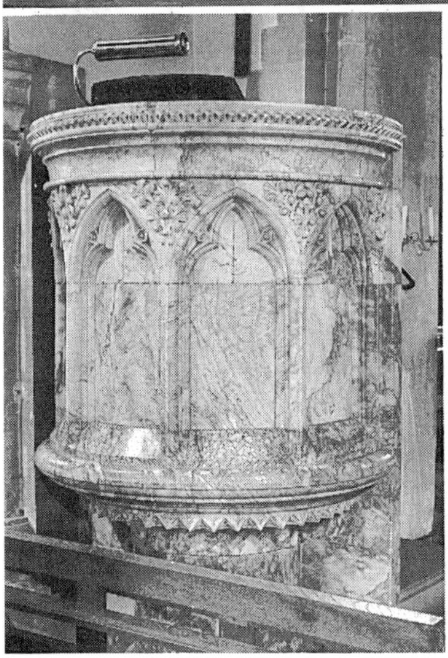

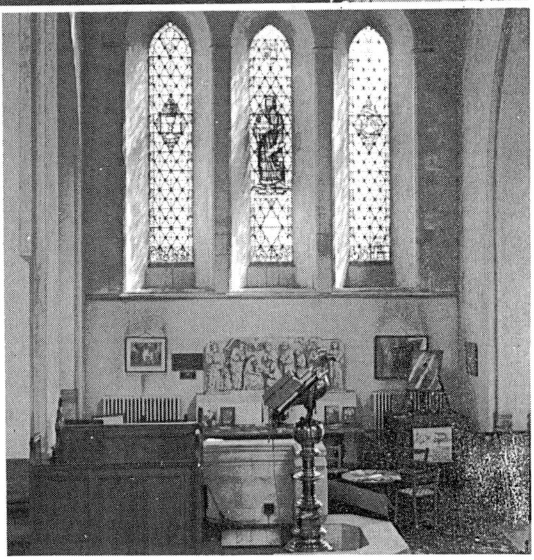

ABOVE: All Saints Church, Denstone, Staffs: reredos.
LEFT: Church of St Peter & Paul, Shiplake, Oxon: pulpit.
(Both NMR) RIGHT: Church of St Mary, Southampton:
sculpture in south transept.

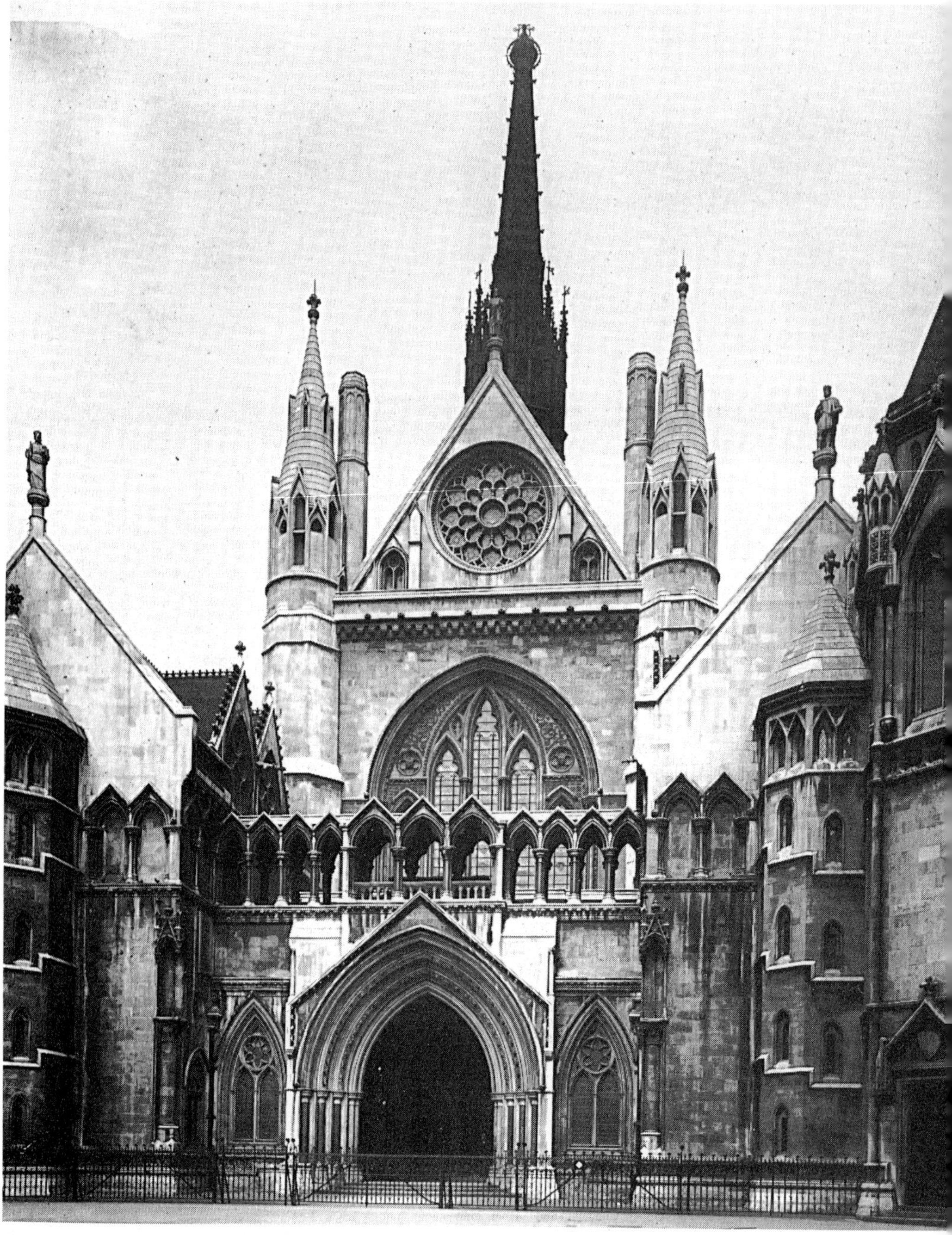

Royal Courts of Justice, London: Solomon and King Alfred are clearly visible to left and right. The figure of Christ is just distinguishable in front of the spiralet. (NMR)

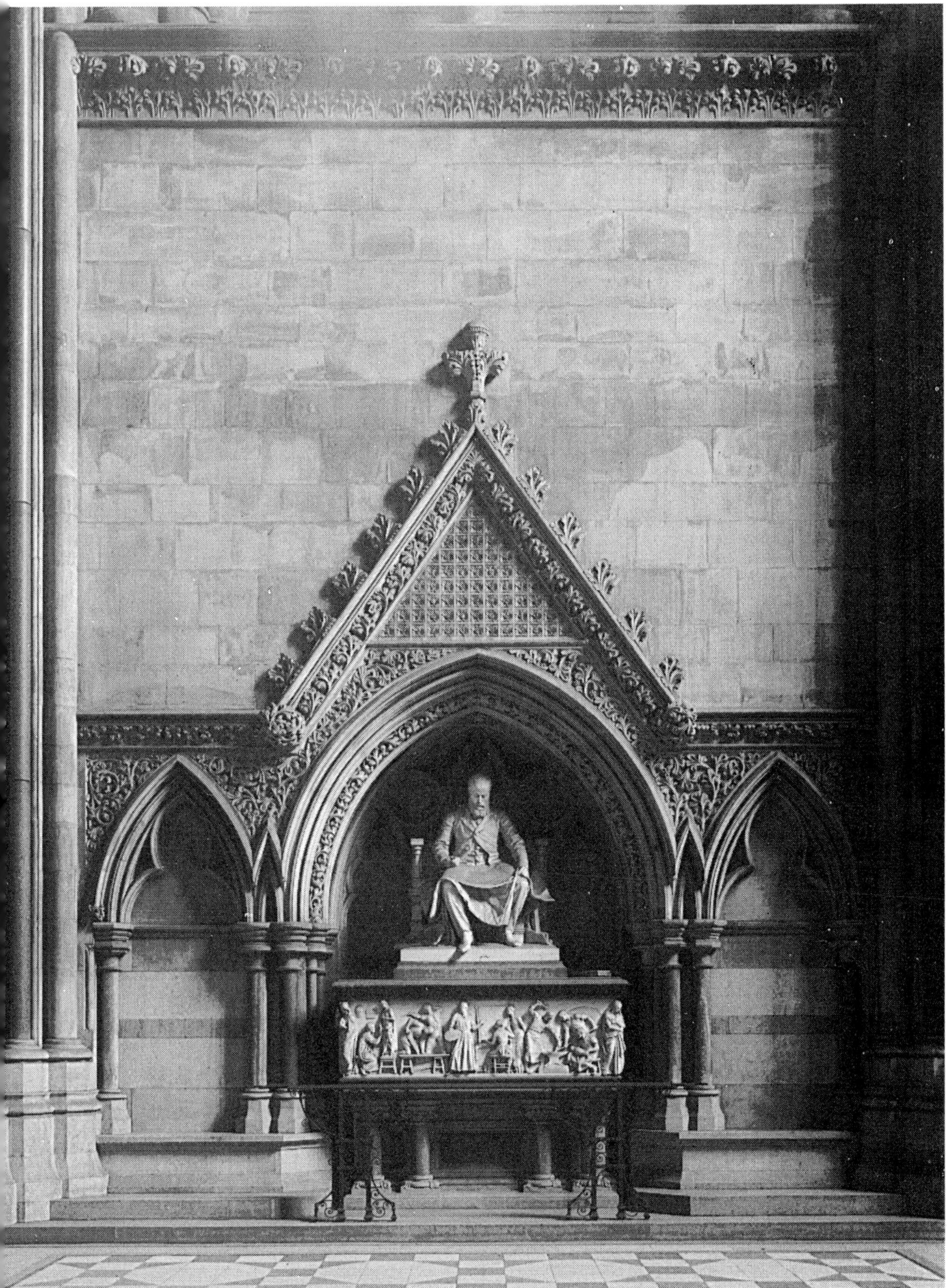

Royal Courts of Justice: monument to George Edmund Street, by H.H. Armstead. (NMR)

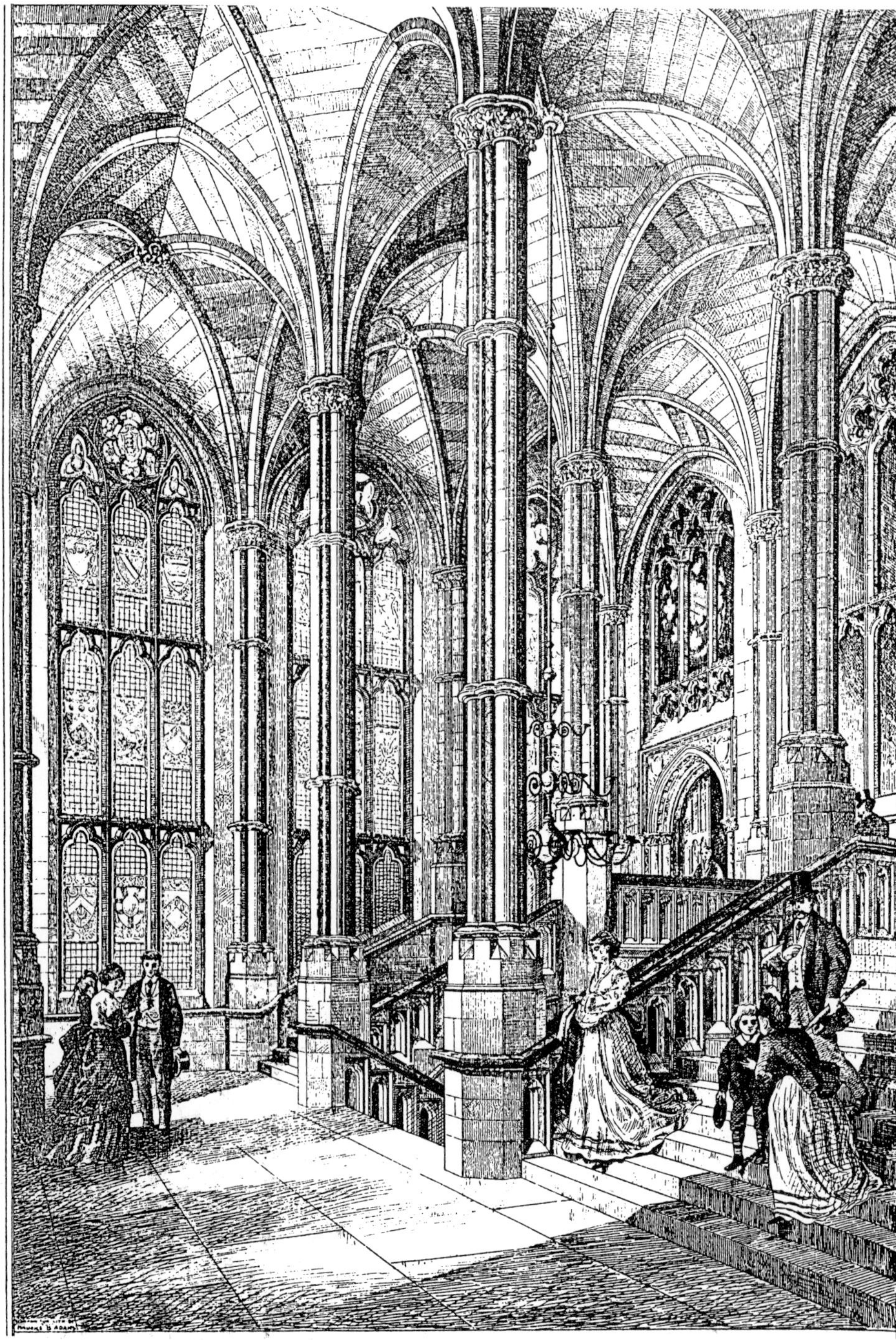

Rochdale Town Hall, Lancashire: view of the Grand Staircase. (RIBA)

New Partners & New Patrons

In 1873 an entry in a directory tells us of a firm Earp and Hobbs, in 63 Lower Mosley Street, Manchester.

Work carried out at Rochdale Town Hall, and at Milnrow and Swinton, also in Lancashire, meant the employment of labour from that region. The Rochdale Town Hall was designed by W.H. Crossland, and the carving of the grand staircase in the entrance hall was Thomas Earp's work. In Manchester itself the Police and Magistrate's Court, designed by Thomas Worthington 1868 – 71, was adorned with decorative stonework by Earp, eliciting the comment 'Ruskinian vitality' by a contemporary critic. St James's Church, Milnrow, designed by Street about 1868, has naturalistic foliage by Thomas Earp ornamenting octagonal piers, as also St Peter's Church, Swinton. In Leek, Staffordshire, the church of St Edward the Confessor has statuary on the pulpit carved by Thomas Earp. St Peter's, Little Aston, Staffs, and Shaw's church in Lower Bentham, Yorkshire, each have an Earp reredos. In his biography of Richard Norman Shaw, Andrew Saint remarks: 'Sculptors of the status of Earp were rare'. Much of this work carried out in the north of England, as well as some work for Scott at St James's Episcopal Church, Edinburgh, suggested a northerly base from which to work, and it appears that Edwin Hobbs, of Moss Side, Manchester emerged as a suitable partner from among the assistants and associates involved in these projects.

Bit by bit Thomas Earp increased his investments and secured his assets by buying or leasing properties in surrounding Lambeth and Camberwell. He already owned, besides the works in Kennington Road, additional workshops in Little Canterbury Place, Lambeth Walk. On the marriage of his son Arthur in 1876, he leased a house for him in Avondale Road, Camberwell. He also purchased the leases of many more properties throughout Camberwell.

Following his son's marriage and the arrival of grandchildren, the firm Earp and Hobbs gradually became known as Earp, Son and Hobbs, although there are no known formal deeds of partnership drawn up before the mid-1880s.

According to some entries in a Poor Rate Book for St Mary's, Lambeth in 1870, Thomas Earp's own house in Kennington Road was assessed at £99 annually. He paid a poor rate at £3 a quarter, a general rate at £1 10s a quarter, police 6d a quarter, sewerage 3s 9d and lighting 7s 6d a quarter.

The census return for 1881 shows him once more as a family man. He had married Ellen Davies, a former machinist probably employed by his sister Emma or one of her associates. She was twenty years his junior and only four years older than his eldest daughter, now married and living away. Second marriages were quite usual in those times, due to early death caused by the health hazards of nineteenth-century sanitation and hygiene.

His marriage to Ellen took place at All Saints Church, Camberwell. We do not know whether any of Thomas Earp's sculptures adorned the surroundings of that ceremony. Ellen's parents, Jacob and Sarah, were present, and Thomas's best man was a Walter Wood. Emily Earp, Thomas's daughter-in-law, was matron of honour. The home of his son Arthur, in Avondale Road, was used as an accommodation address or residence from which the marriage took place, and it is highly probable that a reception was held there afterwards.

The family of his first wife were by now fully independent, married, and raising families of their own. Thomas's hopes for a perpetuation of his businesses were centred upon Arthur, now a junior partner; he also entertained thoughts that Edgar, his only son by Ellen, should also follow this calling. The rest of his second family consisted of four girls — Ethel, Ada, Edith (my mother) and Margaret. Another child, Eveline, had died in infancy.

At the beginning of Thomas Earp's career, George Myers and his craftsmen, of which Earp was one, were associated with William Butterfield in the building of All Saints, Margaret Street, London.

This was the work by which Butterfield achieved public acclaim. He was born in 1814 and studied architecture in Worcester, where he made a study of the cathedral. He became involved with the Cambridge Camden (afterwards the Ecclesiological) Society and was appointed an agent for that Society's scheme for the improvement of church plate and other accessories. He went on to design buildings, including St Albans, Holborn, Balliol College Chapel, and Merton and Keble Colleges. He also did much restoration of existing buildings.

He had his own personal idiosyncrasies and definite tastes, reflected in his attitudes. By contrast to Street and Scott his churchmanship, according to the *Dictionary of National Biography* was 'based on something deeper than ceremonial. He had no liking for elaborate ritualism. He tended to persuade those who regularly worked for him to share his own scruples against any work for the Roman Catholic Church'.

His work was mainly in the medium of plain brickwork, achieving its effect with contrasting colours, often resulting in great exuberance. He made little use of decorative sculpture and what ornaments his churches possessed were additions often endowed by patrons. Thomas Earp had several contracts of this kind, including a wooden pulpit at St Mary's, Battle, near Hastings; a pulpit at St Augustine's, South Kensington, a pulpit in Christ Church, Albany Street and a reredos at St Mary's, Warwick.

Two of these works are worth describing. St Augustine's interior is wholly impressive, and the octagonal-shaped pulpit is in white marble with recessed arches, supported by blue marble columns and standing on a blue base. It was presented to the church by a member of the congregation, which explains its presence. It was intended as a thank-offering in grateful memory of the teaching of Richard Robert Chope BA, the first vicar in 1865. Inside the top of the pulpit is the inscription: 'We preach Christ crucified unto them which are called. Christ the Power of God and the Wisdom of God'.

Christ Church, Albany Street, London, was built in 1837 to a classical design by Sir James Pennethorne. It had been used by the first Anglican religious community in England, started by Dr Pusey in 1845, and many distinguished preachers had been heard there: Archdeacon Manning (later a Cardinal), Dr Pusey and John Keble. Between 1849 and 1884 William Butterfield designed various items of interior decoration, including a lectern, pavements, a font, altar-piece and reredos. In 1870 a window, designed by Dante Gabriel Rossetti and executed by William Morris, was installed. The Rossetti family had worshipped there ever since 1843, and Christine Rossetti was a district visitor in neighbouring Old Robert Street. Dr Pusey's sister presented the jewelled chalice. A copy of Raphael's 'Transfiguration' from the Vatican was placed in the east end in 1840. In more recent years, Daphne du Maurier was baptised in the church in 1907 and George Orwell was buried from there in 1950. The house which became the vicarage was where from Mendelssohn first performed, on a piano, the music of *Elijah.*

Here the pulpit, of hexagonal shape, was executed by Thomas Earp in alabaster and is a memorial to Georgina Fox (1809-1883) and was dedicated 'to her good works to the glory of God in this parish'.

Not the most successful work for a Butterfield restoration was the reredos of St Mary's, Warwick. The sculpted figures in the three panels depicting New Testament scenes have been garishly coloured, resulting in a tawdry effect and probably spoiling the quality the work originally possessed. The pulpit in wood at St Mary's, Battle, is competent and pleasing, being typical of Butterfield's taste and requirements. To quote Paul Thompson in *The Biography of William Butterfield,* 'We can well believe that Butterfield rejected the doctrine of Ruskin and William Morris that free craftsmanship was essential to the spirit of Gothic architecture...he was opposed to the new cult of letting the workman think and act for himself'.

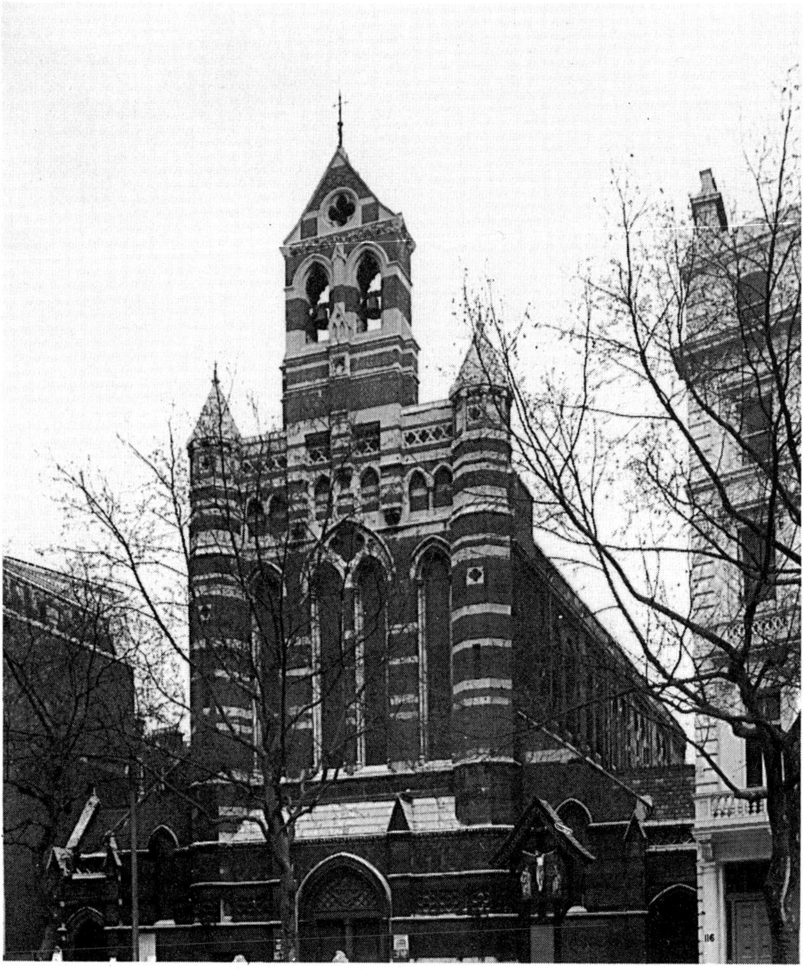

Church of St Augustine, South Kensington, London.
View from west. (NMR)

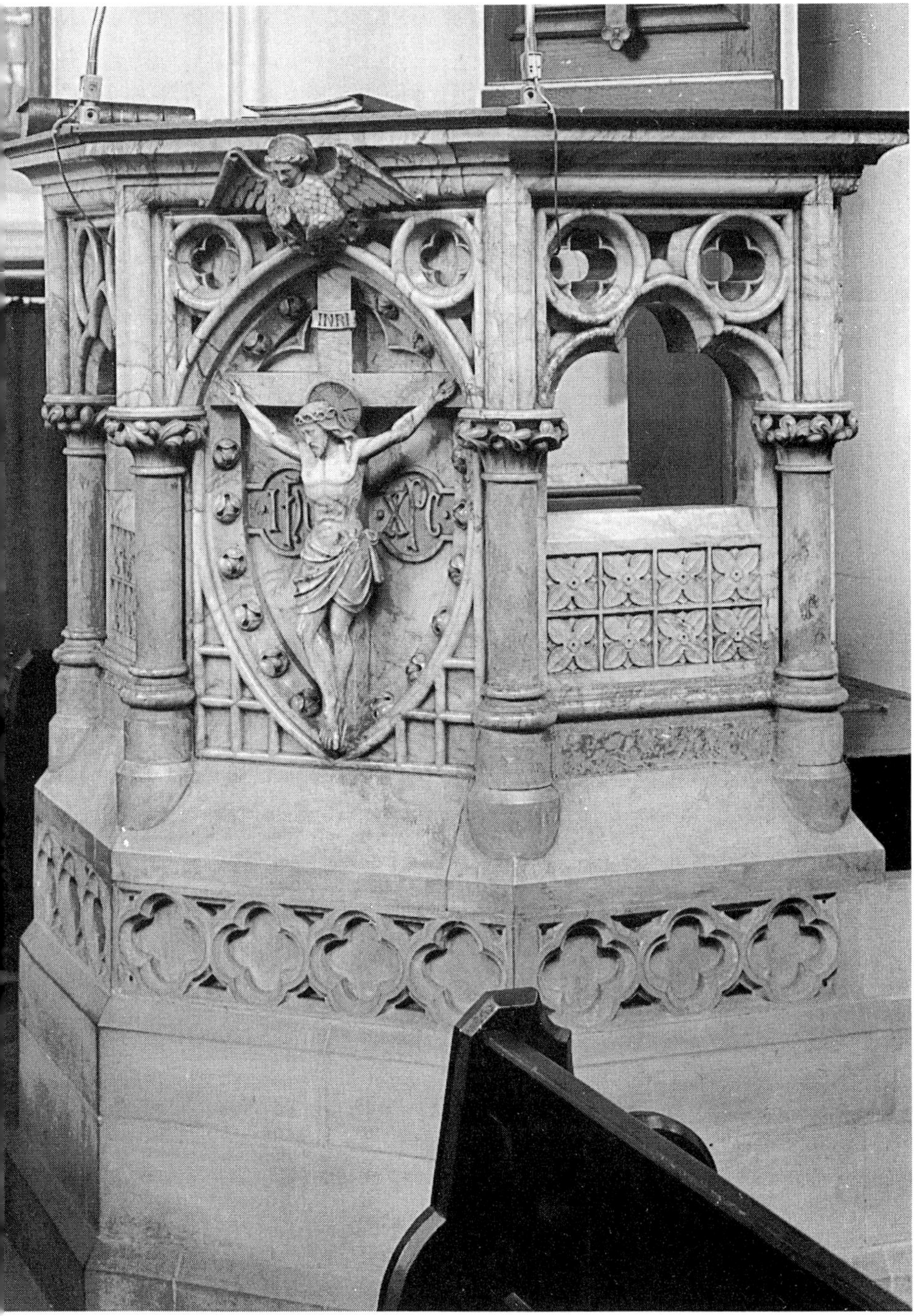

Church of St Augustine, South Kensington, London: pulpit. (NMR)

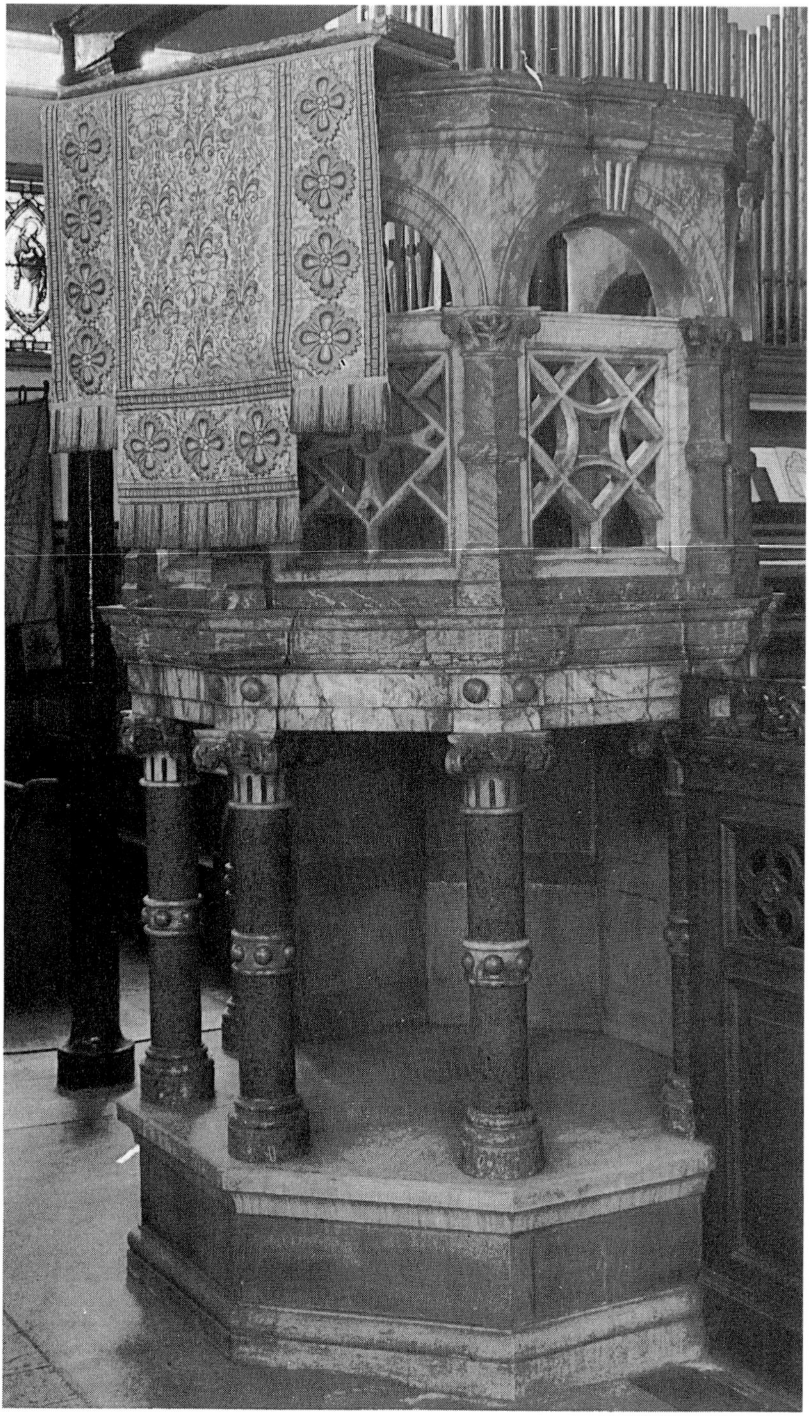

Christ Church, Albany Street, London: pulpit. (NMR)

Times of Change

Although Street had died, the workshops of Thomas Earp and his partners still had plenty of post-humous contracts to be completed for him and his trustees. Among these is the screen in the chapel of Eton College. Standing between the ante-chapel and the chapel proper, it serves to support the organ. It is in close proximity to the famous wall paintings, depicting miraculous events attributed to the Blessed Virgin. Nearby also is Sir Galahad by G.F. Watts, and the Star of Bethlehem tapestry of Morris & Co, designed by Burne-Jones. This work was done in 1882.

Street's famous pupil, Richard Norman Shaw, continued his master's patronage of Thomas Earp. Shaw was already noted for developing new styles of urban domestic housing in the company of Philip Webb and Eden Nesfield. Much of his work was in the suburban expansion south-east of London towards Bromley, Bickley and Chislehurst – notably alterations to Charlton House, the home of Mrs Craik (of *John Halifax* fame) at Shortlands, and a fine house in the Queen Anne style at West Wickham. He is most famous for 'New' Scotland Yard on the Thames Embankment (now a Government Office).

In his church of St Swithin, Bournemouth, begun in 1875 and completed about 1891, the high altar reredos was executed by Earp, affording a distinctive feature in the wide, aisleless, barn-like nave.

Sir Arthur Blomfield designed the tomb for the seventeenth-century Bishop Pearson in Chester Cathedral which Thomas Earp carved in 1863. It stands in the north transept, amongst other work by Blomfield, such as the Italian Quattrocento-style bust of Thomas Brassey in the south choir aisle and the tablet to Bishop Jacobson in the north choir aisle. Blomfield had also done restoration work to St Werburgh's shrine in the lady chapel of the cathedral.

Thomas Earp also did some carving for Blomfield in the church of St Jude in South London (since destroyed in World War II) and a school in Bedfordbury, near Covent Garden; this has since been demolished.

However, there is some outstanding work by Thomas Earp in Blomfield's Church of the Holy Trinity at Gosport, the campanile of which is a noteworthy landmark, clearly visible from the

Portsmouth side of the harbour. According to Pevsner, it had been built originally as a chapel-of-ease to Alverstoke in 1686 and completely restored by Blomfield in 1887, with the development of Gosport as a naval dormitory town. Beneath the barrel roof of the nave can be seen the font and pulpit, executed by Earp in coloured marble and alabaster. This church contains an organ upon which Handel played — not at Gosport, but at Canons Park, North London. It was moved in the middle 1700s.

In 1888 Thomas Earp completed the decorations of the Sodality Chapel in Stonyhurst, Lancashire. This was part of the growth and development of this Catholic public school which the Society of Jesus had founded in 1794, after their expulsion from France.

The house known as Stonyhurst existed since the fourteenth century under the lords of the manor, the Shireburns. During the eighteenth century a daughter of that family married the Duke of Norfolk. This was followed by several more changes of ownership until the Jesuits took over.

The Order was responsible for vast extensions as the school was caught up in the public school boom. Like Downside, it was part of the successful attempt to show that rich Catholic families could enjoy the same education as the rest of the èlite.

The designer of much of the nineteenth-century work at the school was a member of the Jesuit Order, the noted Fr Richard Vaughan. J.J. Scoles, of Farm Street, designed some other early work, and there is some influence from Norman Shaw in later work. The Sodality Chapel, built in 1856, was by C.A. Buckler. It is a long, aisleless building to the north of the refectory. The decorations that Thomas Earp completed thirty years later (doubtless without the knowledge of William Butterfield) depicted angels and saints, and called for a mention in a later edition of the *History of the Gothic Revival.*

This was not the only part of Lancashire where the Lambeth sculptor was to leave his mark. In Liverpool, the church of St Mary has an Earp reredos designed by Street, while at Walton, a suburb of Liverpool, in the church of St John the Evangelist, Earp carved a frame for a reredos by Woolner, the Pre-Raphaelite sculptor.

A more modest work can be found in South London in the Church of the Ascension, Arthur Cawston's first church, where Thomas Earp's Crucifixion reredos is the only outstanding piece of ornamentation in an interior otherwise sparsely decorated. It was endowed by a Mrs Pugh of Clapham Common, in memory of her husband in 1888.

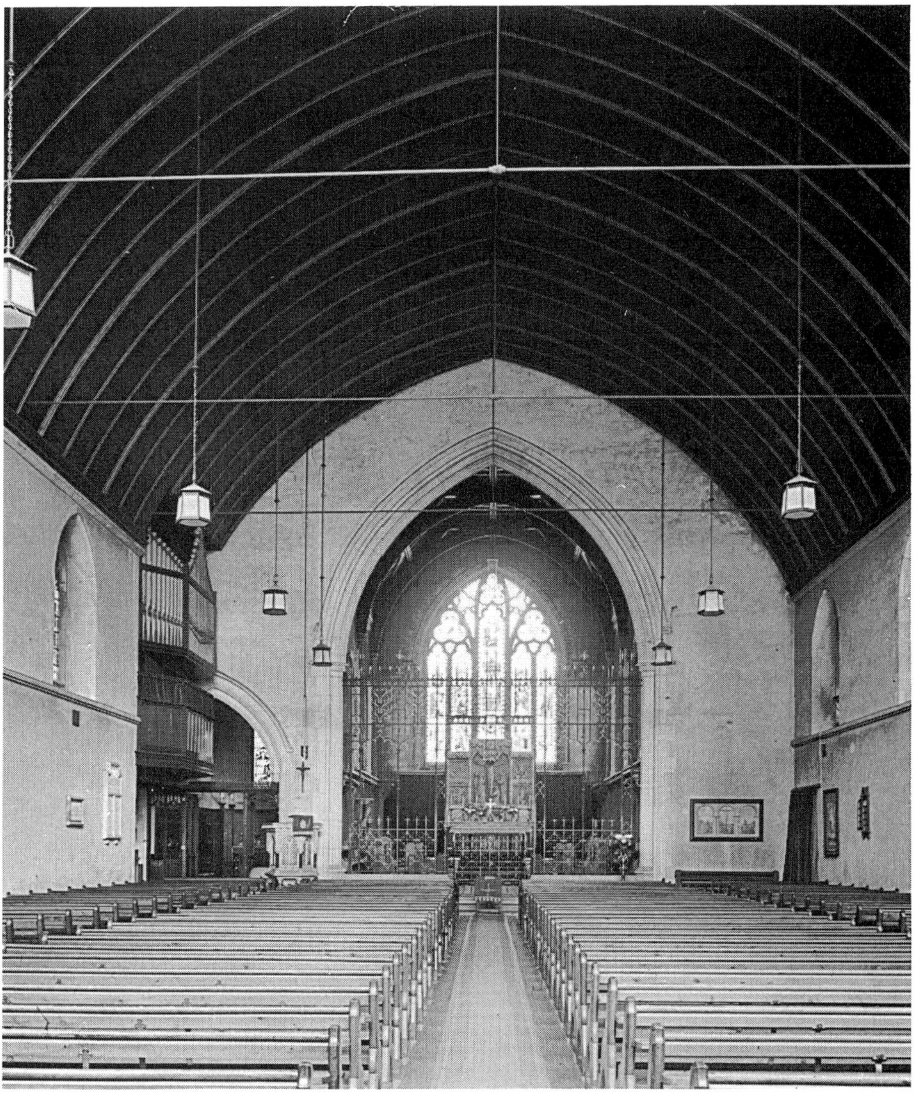

Church of St Swithin, Bournemouth: view of nave, with Earp's reredos at the far end. (NMR)

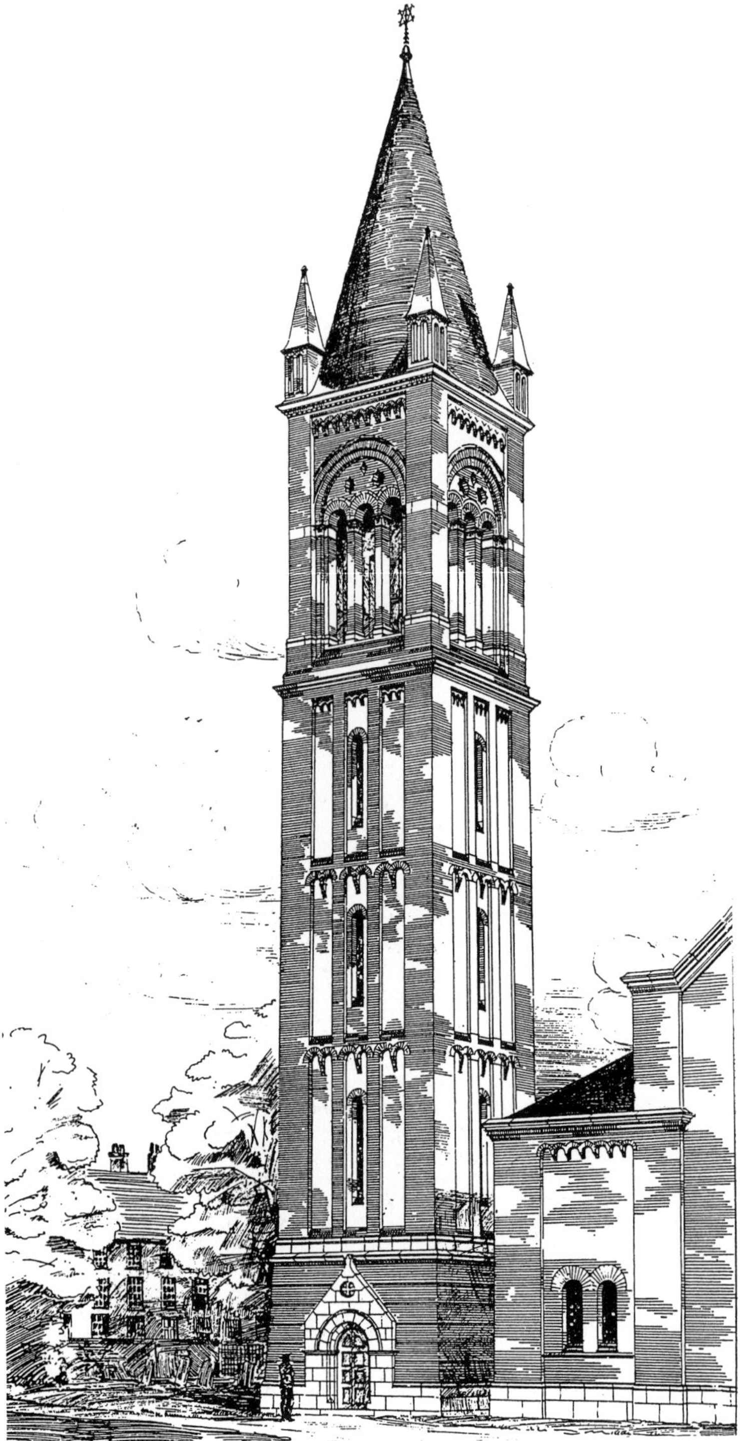

Holy Trinity Church, Gosport, Hants: the Campanile.
(BN)

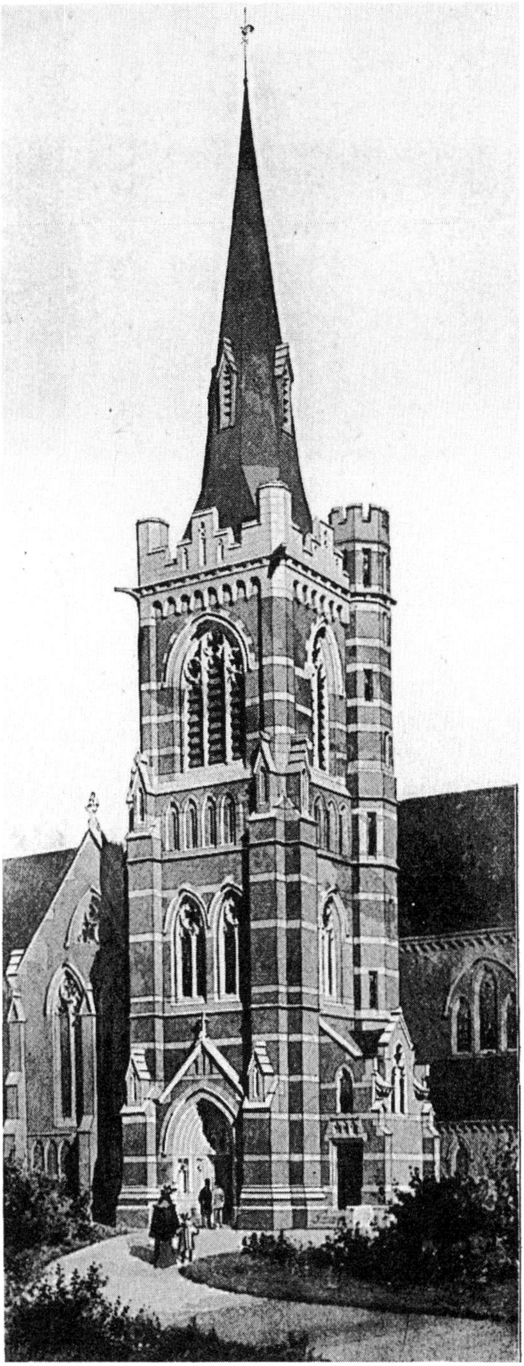

Church of the Ascension, Balham, London. (NMR)

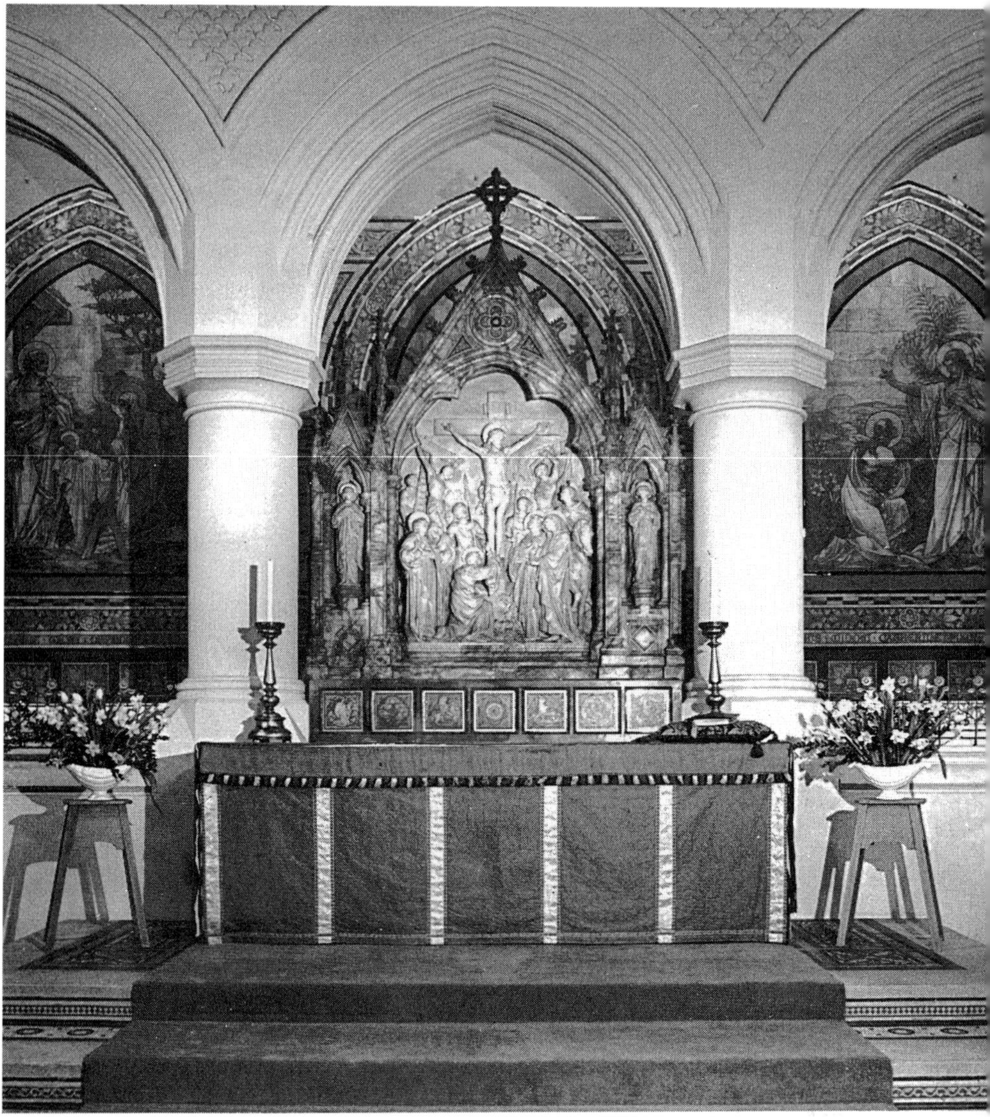

Church of the Ascension, Balham: reredos. (NMR)

SOME SCENES REVISITED

About 1860 a new parish was established in 'the poor and populous district of Notting Dale, West London', a location for some striking work by Thomas Earp.

A certain Father Henry Augustus Rawes was instructed by Cardinal Wiseman, Archbishop of Westminster, to choose a site for a church in a space near the end of Pottery Lane, West London. This area was characterised by potteries and brickfields and peopled by Irish immigrants who added pig-keeping to the local trades, and by other tradespeople and families displaced from elsewhere by the building of railways and new roads.

The church was dedicated to St Francis of Assisi, and it was paid for almost entirely by Father Rawes himself, and he engaged the architect Henry Clutton to draw up the plans. Clutton was brilliantly assisted by John Bentley, who later became famous for his cathedral at Westminster. They jointly employed Thomas Earp to undertake interior decorative carving.

The church was built in a severely simple style 'imposed by the poverty of the neighborhood', but austerity was relieved by light from stained glass windows and stonework in alabaster inlaid with glass and paintings by Westlake, exuberantly carved by Thomas Earp.

In later days the people of St Francis make their own contribution to the gaiety and festivities of the annual Notting Hill Carnival.

During 1856 Thomas Earp carved a pulpit for a church dedicated to St Margaret, in Bodelwydden, North Wales.

The church owes its construction to Lady Margaret Willoughby de Broke, widow of Henry Peyton, 16th Baron Willoughby de Broke, who had died in 1852.

After her husband's death Lady Margaret obtained the approval of the Bishop of St Asaph to build a parish church for her own home village of Bodelwydden, separate from St Asaph's.

Architect John Gibson, a pupil of Hansom and an associate of Barry, was commissioned to design the work. The church was built of native limestone, but its furnishings were executed lavishly by Earp in fourteen different varieties of marble, including some of French, Belgian, Sicilian and Irish origin. As a consequence the church came to be known as 'the marble church'.

A feature of the church is the hammer-beam roof constructed entirely of oak without a single nail – only wooden pegs were used.

Thomas Earp's pulpit was the gift of Emma and Harriet, two sisters of Lady Margaret. It comprises five panels depicting Christ and the four Evangelists.

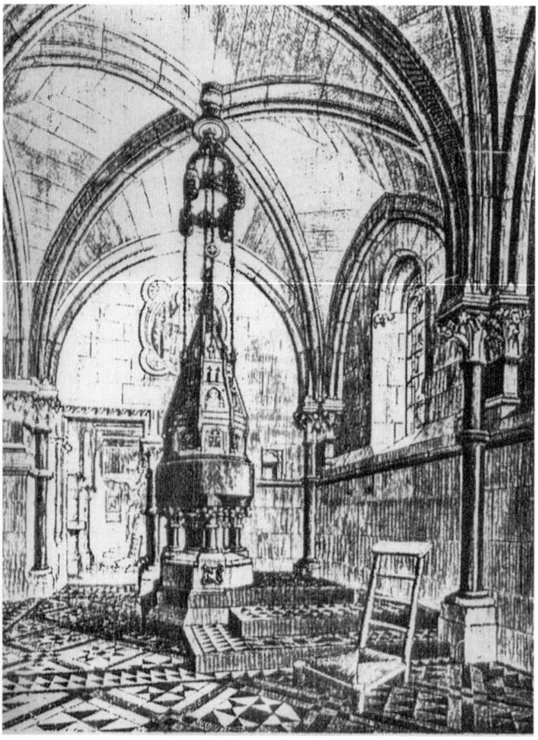

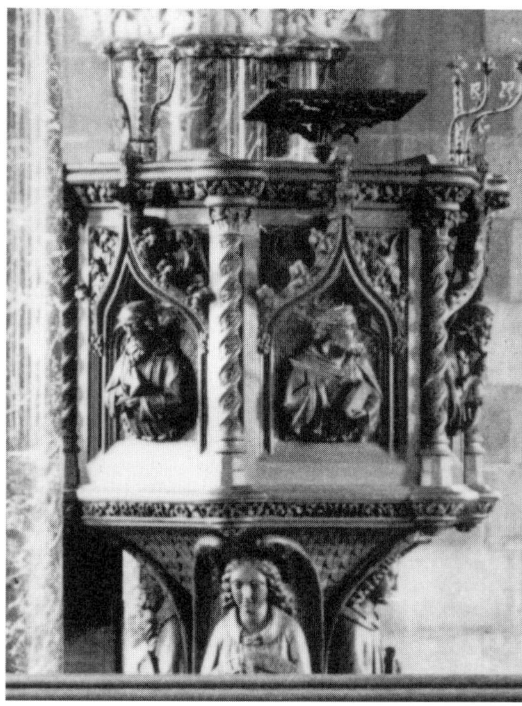

ABOVE: St Francis of Assisi, Notting Hill: Baptistry, showing Earp's carvings at base of font. BELOW: St Margaret's Church, Bodelwydden: the font. (NMRW)

Sermons in Stone

A church was built at Whitechapel, London, at about 1877 and dedicated to St Mary. Features of the church which deserve special mention include a font and a pulpit, both of which were the work of Thomas Earp.

The pulpit is of Derbyshire alabaster. On the two sides are four square panels depicting the four Evangelists, together with their appropriate emblems. On the panel on the south side, next to the steps, is carved a lily, the symbol of Mary's virginity. Beneath the bookrest at the front is a representation of the Angel with the sealed book, mentioned in Revelations.

Caen stone was used in the provision of the font. At the four angles are carved figures of Isaiah, Ezekiel, Joel, and Zacharia, the four prophets who foretold the baptism. In between, on three of the faces, are a foliated cross, and a dove and a pelican, creatures of great scriptural and mystical significance.

A contemporary journal commented: 'The whole impresses the thoughtful observer as truly a "sermon in stone"'.

Nothing remains of this work today. St Mary's was completely destroyed in a bombing raid in 1940.

During 1870 Thomas Earp was commissioned to provide a reredos of alabaster as part of restorations to St Asaph's Cathedral in Clwyd, North Wales.

St Asaph's was founded in the reign of Edward I in the early English style. Towards the end of the eighteenth century and during the early part of the nineteenth this cathedral underwent considerable restorations caused by years of neglect. The old chapter house was demolished in 1779 and the choir began to be remodelled. In 1780 the east window was restored.

Between 1809 and 1832 work on the choir was completed and many other alterations were made to the roodscreen and cross-arches. These infuriated the Cathedral administrators and their consultants. Sir George Scott was called to give an appraisal, and observed that the situation resulted in an inordinate overcrowding of choir and chancel, leaving nave and transept virtually useless.

Scott was allowed to plan a complete restoration of the cathedral to make it fully usable for Christian worship according to Tractarian principles in the Church of England. Scott also wanted to exemplify prevalent architectural ideas. Generous donors made it possible to enrich the furnishings for liturgical purposes.

The chancel roof was restored with panelled oak, and the floor paved with tiling. The new High Altar with Thomas Earp's reredos was established in the east end. The figurework represents the procession of Christ to Calvary.

The entire restoration was completed about 1870.

St Peter's Church, Broadstairs, was enriched in 1867–68 by a new reredos for the High Altar carved by Thomas Earp.

The money for this was raised by subscription in the parish by a Mr Thomas Gray, whose family was one of the oldest in the parish.

The reredos is ornamented with two quatrefoils, one containing a marble cross and the other depicting angels bearing shields. Surrounding carvings suggest harvest and vineyard motifs. The Creed, Lord's Prayer and the Commandments are painted on oil panels. Marble and alabaster are used in the dado and cornices, and the paintings and mosaics are the work of Messrs Heaton, Butler and Bayne.

In a former farmyard at Ridley, some six miles south of Gravesend, Kent, is a small church dedicated to St Peter. In 1869, the rector, Thomas Frankard Phelps, decided to complete a reconstruction begun some ten years earlier. Robert Pope, the London architect, submitted drawings for a new chancel, of which the central point was to be the reredos depicting the Last Supper.

Pope introduced Thomas Earp, noted for his stone-and-alabaster pulpit in the church in Stone nearby, described in a previous chapter. Earp demurred at the proposed design, as the available space, which was a small trifoliate niche $2\frac{1}{2}$ feet broad by 2 feet high, was too small to accommodate the customary 12 or 13 figures. He suggested the Crucifixion instead.

Dr Phelps objected. He was of Tractarian inclinations, regarding the Holy Communion as the heart of Christian worship, and the Last Supper, in his belief, was in fact the First Holy Communion.

Earp did as he was asked, overcoming the difficulty of limitations of space by carving the figures in smaller and more intricate detail than was his usual style.

Each of the 13 faces was not more than an inch and a half long; the embroidery of the tablecloth was executed with great delicacy, the hands and feet were anatomically correct; together with the clothing and furnishings the workmanship of Earp is revealed at its best.

In 1884 the church of St Augustine, Ramsgate, Kent, was provided with an altar-piece designed by Peter Paul Pugin, the son of Augustus Welby Pugin. The carving was done by Thomas Earp.

St Augustine's was among the first of the churches designed by the elder Pugin, and was started in 1844. Due to lack of funds it was not finished in his lifetime, and the work was only brought to completion by his son forty years later.

The altar-piece was originally a main feature of the sanctuary until after 1960 when, due to liturgical changes decreed by the Second Vatican Council, Earp's High Altar was removed from the sanctuary and set up in the North Cloister.

A remarkable pulpit by Thomas Earp is the focal point of the Union Chapel, Islington, north London, which was built in 1877 by James Cubitt. The style 'Union' is because the first congregation which gathered in this place consisted of both evangelical Anglicans and Non-conformists.

It was the year of the French Revolution, and many Christians were concerned to heal some of their divisions in the face of new and uncertain ideologies threatening to destabilise society.

Cubitt designed the chapel to a plan based on an Italian Romanesque style, and it was octagonal in shape. However, he put in stone mouldings and arches which are French in form, and the pulpit is a traditional design usually associated with Victorian Gothic. The details of the pulpit would have been designed by Earp himself, as he was familiar with this style.

It stands above the platform at the front of the chapel, as is usual in evangelical places of worship. It is mounted on a base of Caen stone, while the steps are in Portland stone which is more hard-wearing. The copings are of English alabaster, supported on columns of Mexican onyx, below which are heads of Church Fathers and later Reformers in Tottenhoe stone. Arches between the sides have columns of onyx and Verde Antica green marble. Panels of Egyptian onyx and Greek Cipolino marble are adorned with diamond and circular patterns.

Altogether there are ten different sorts of stone in the design.

The pulpit is so positioned that the preacher is able to see and address every member of the congregation.

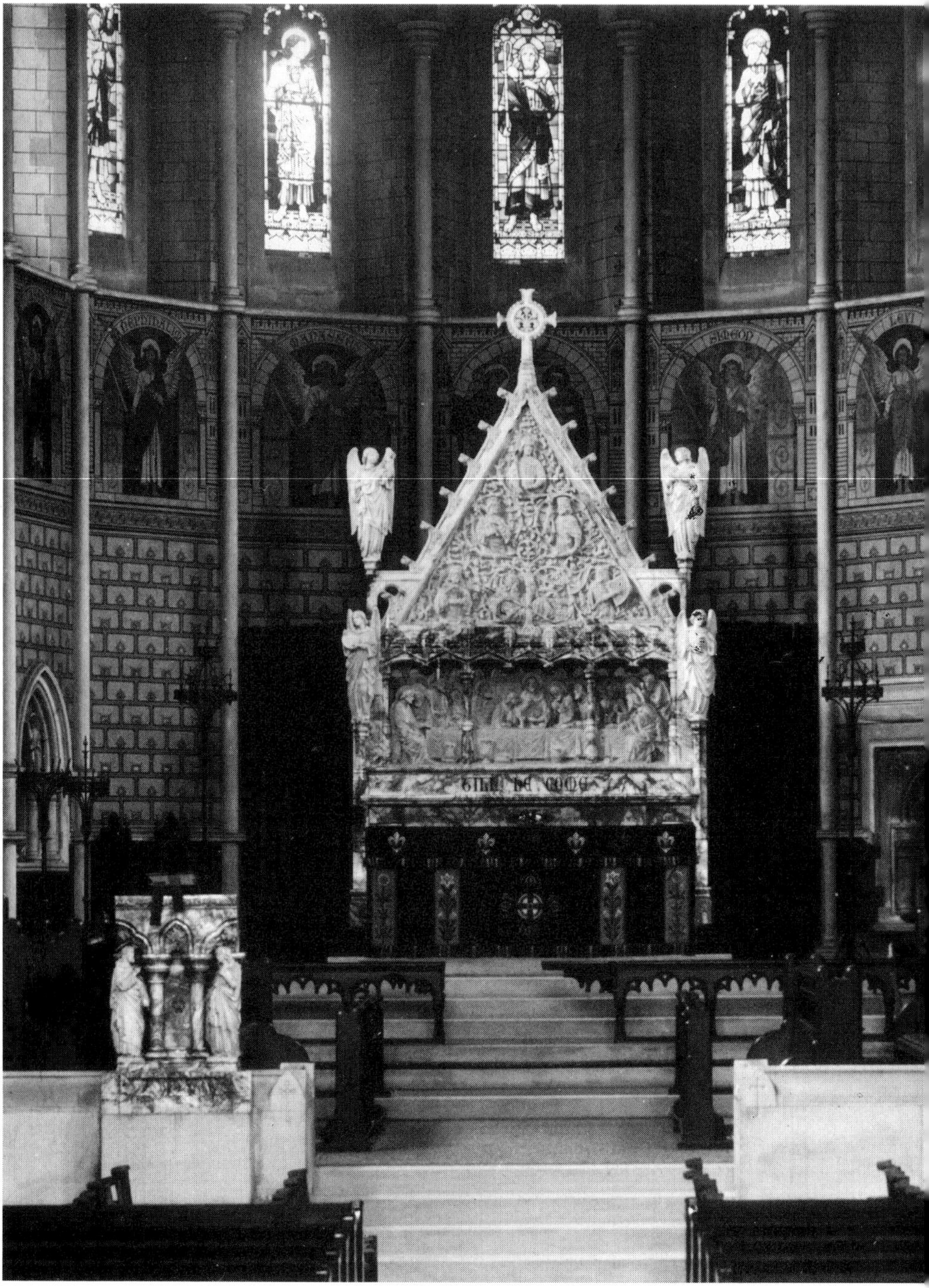

St Mary's Church, Whitechapel: reredos by Earp. (EHNMR)

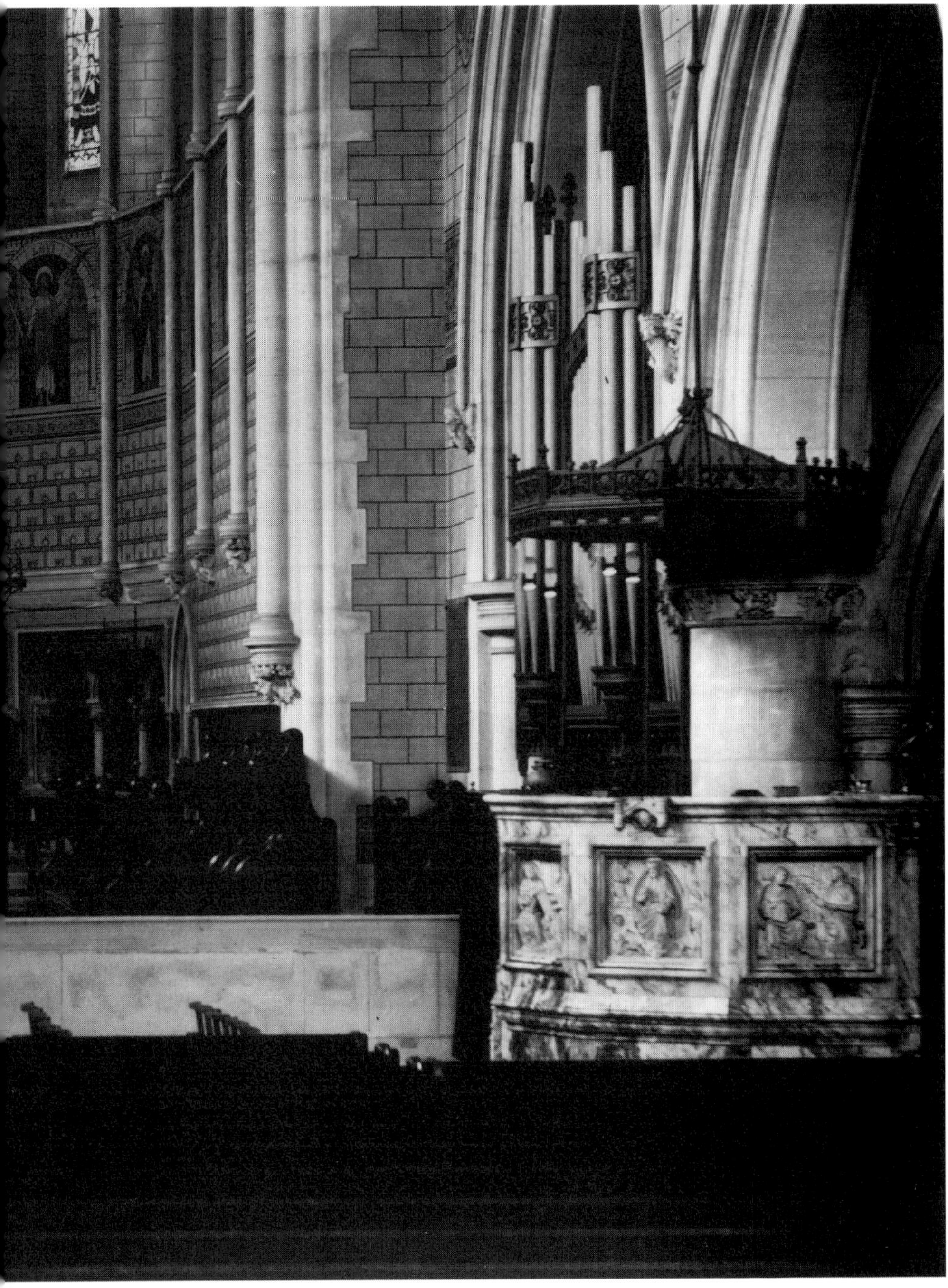

St Mary's Church, Whitechapel: Earp's pulpit. (EHNMR)

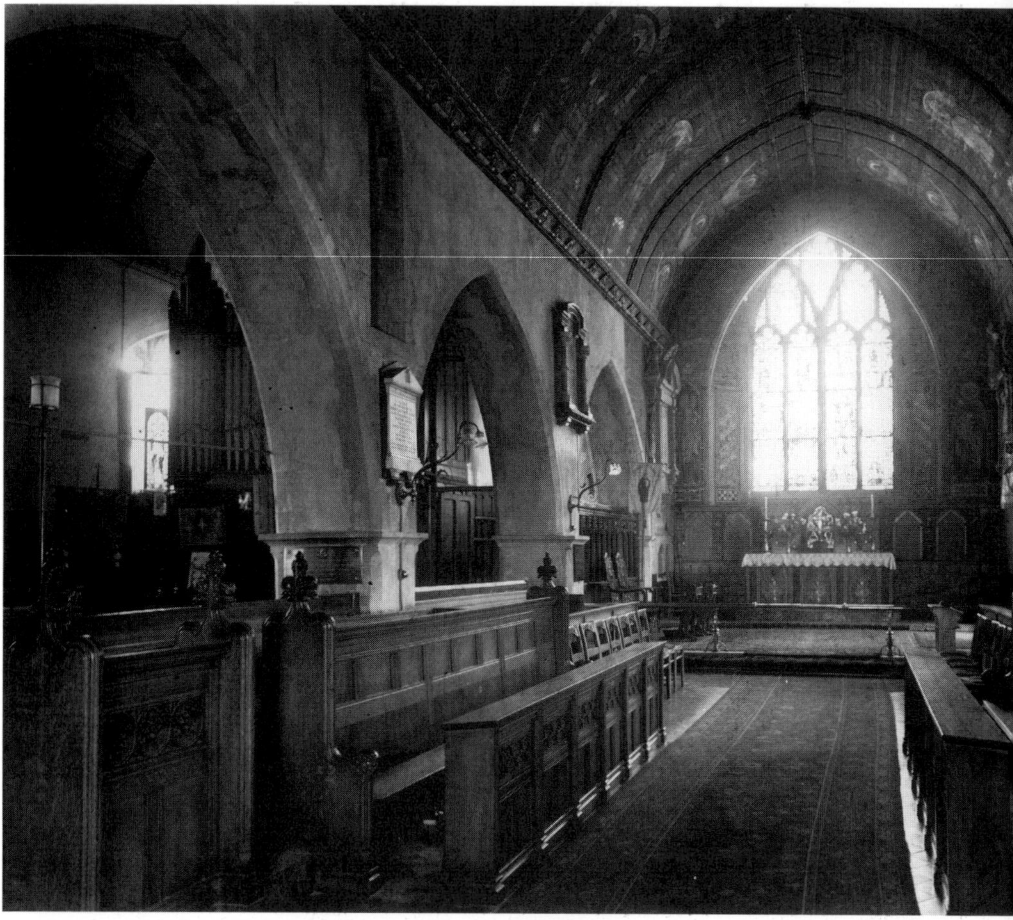

St Peter's, Broadstairs: the chancel and reredos.
(EHNMR)

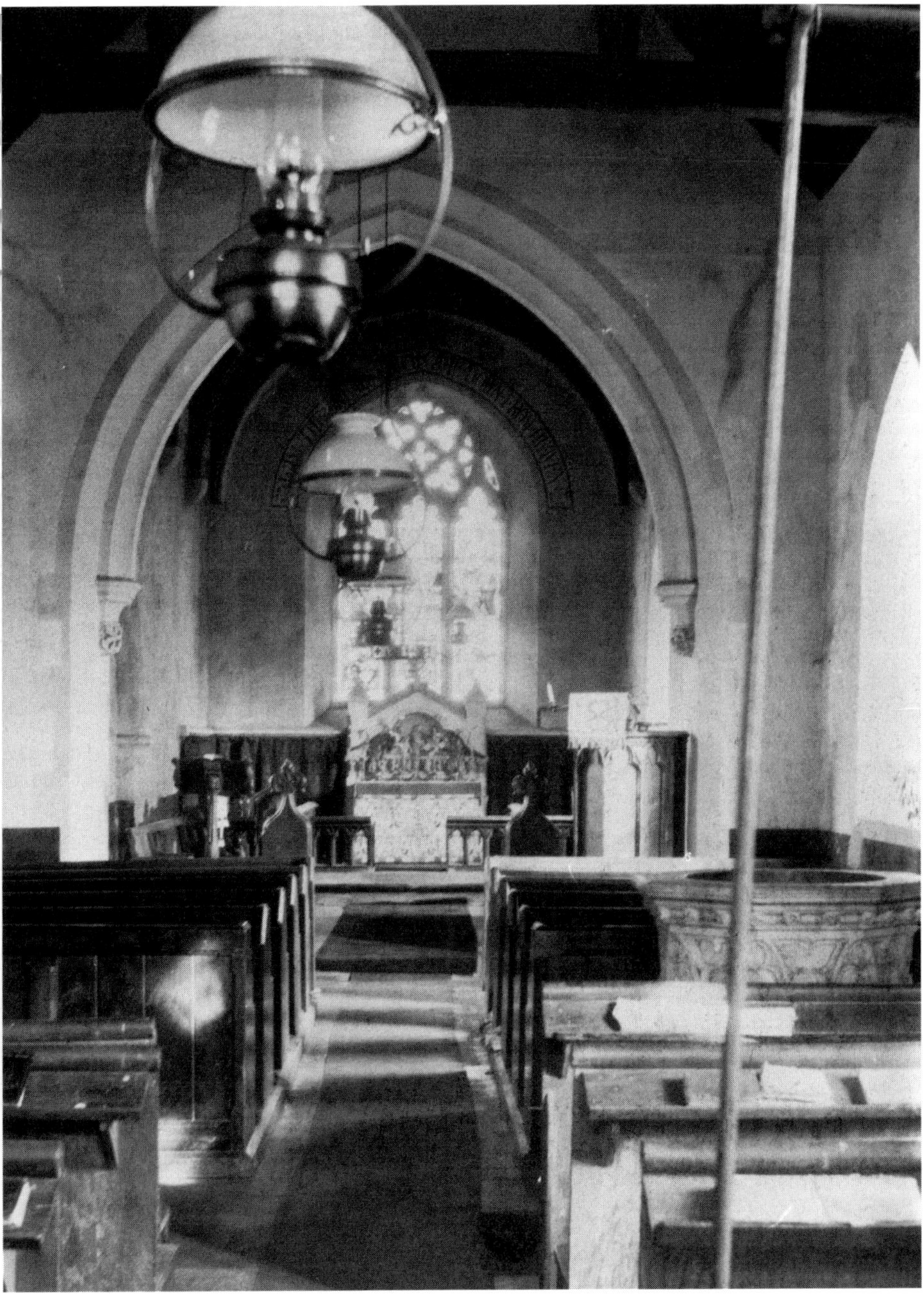

St Peter's Church, Ridley, Kent: the chancel and reredos. (EHNMR)

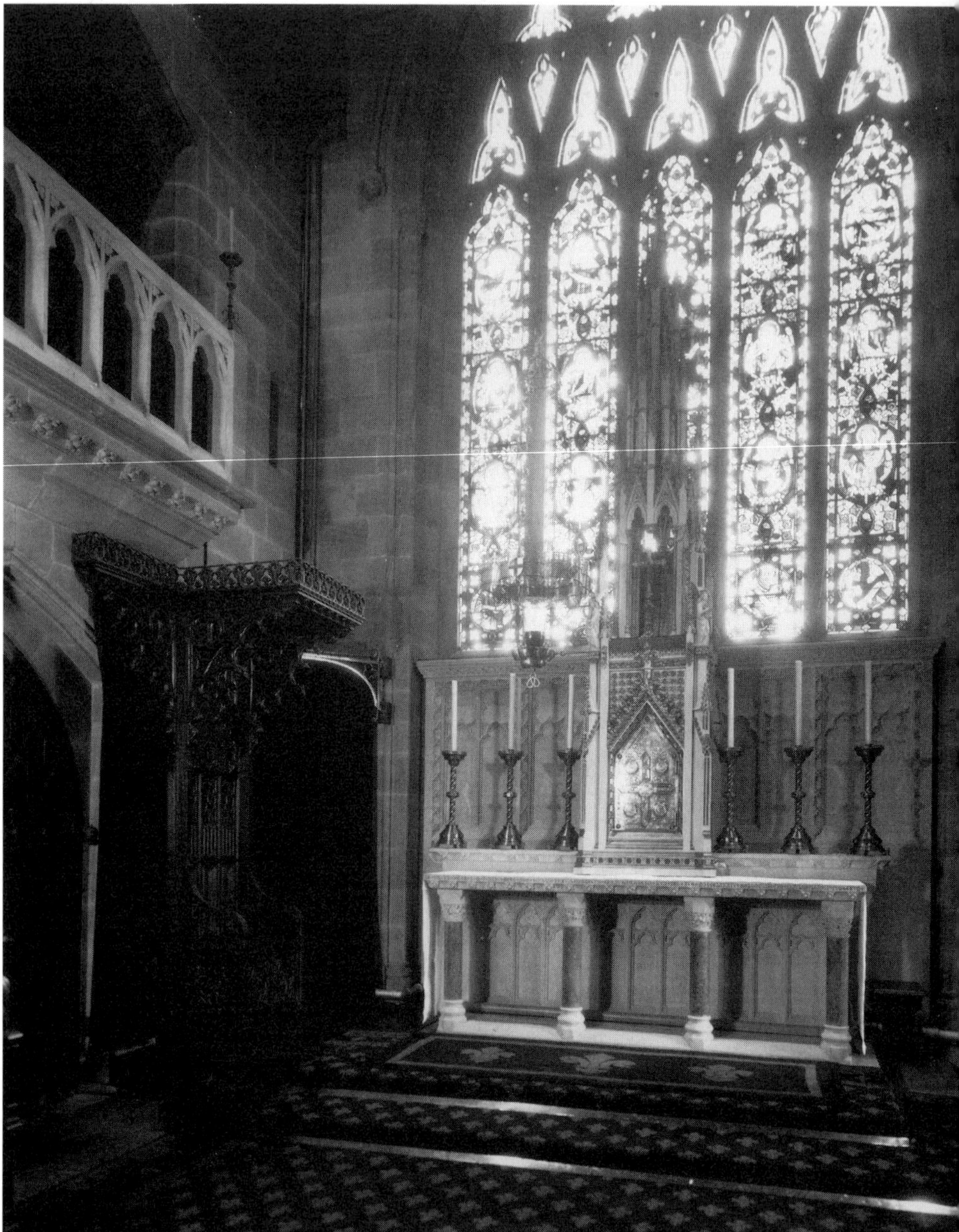

St Augustine's, Ramsgate: the Pugin altar, carved by Earp. (EHNMR)

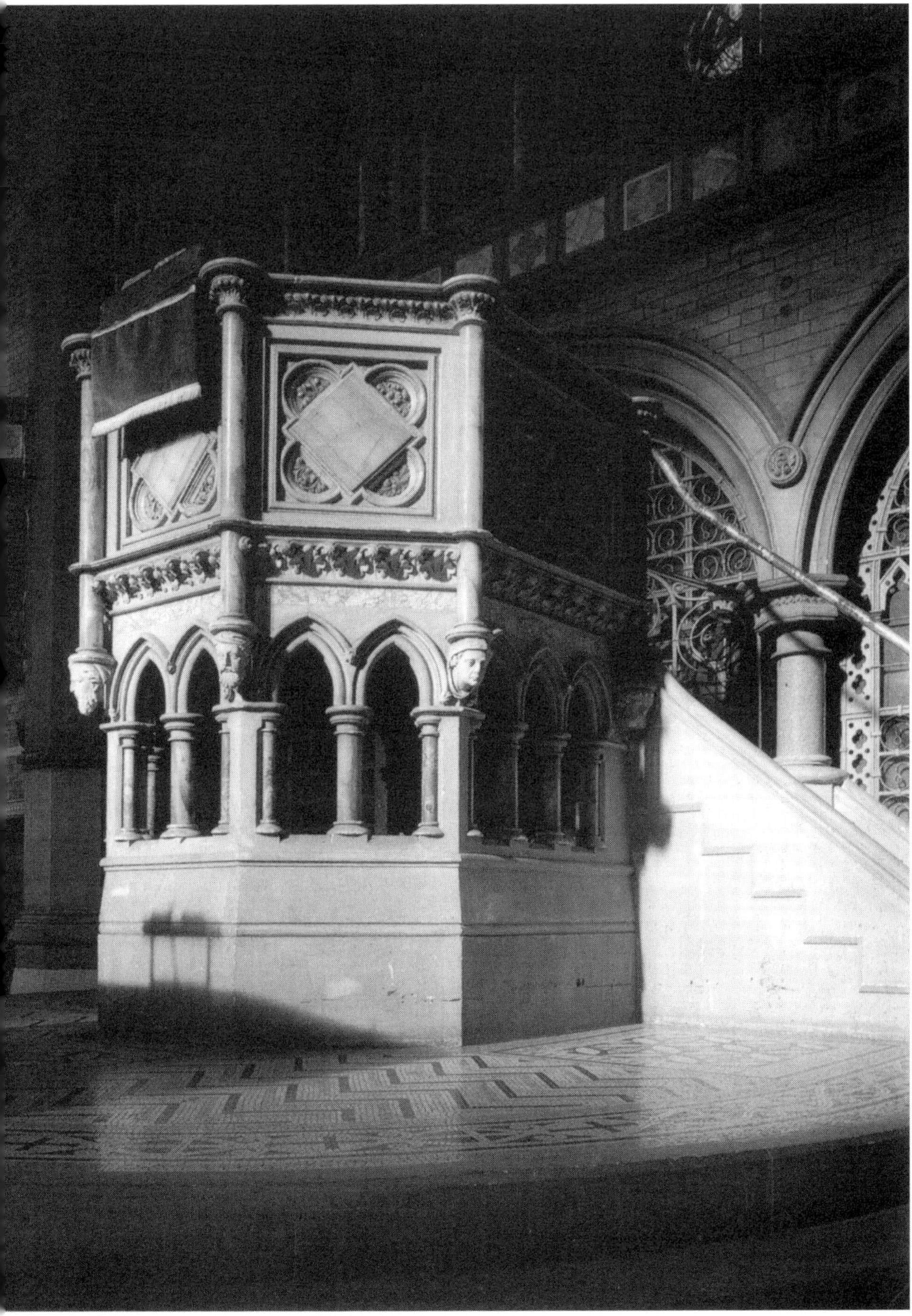

Union Chapel, Islington: Cubitt's pulpit, carved by Earp. (PL/FUC)

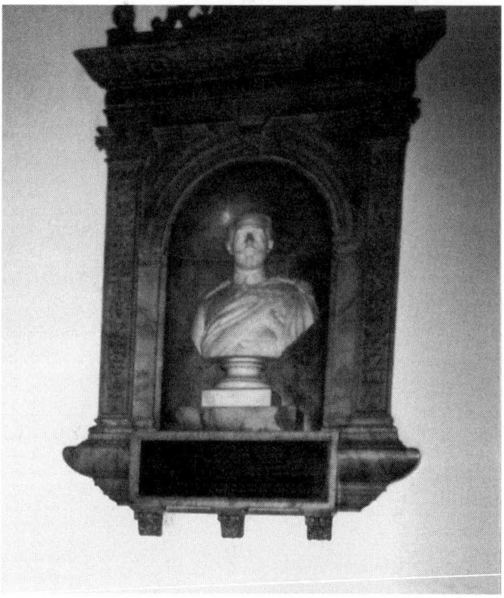

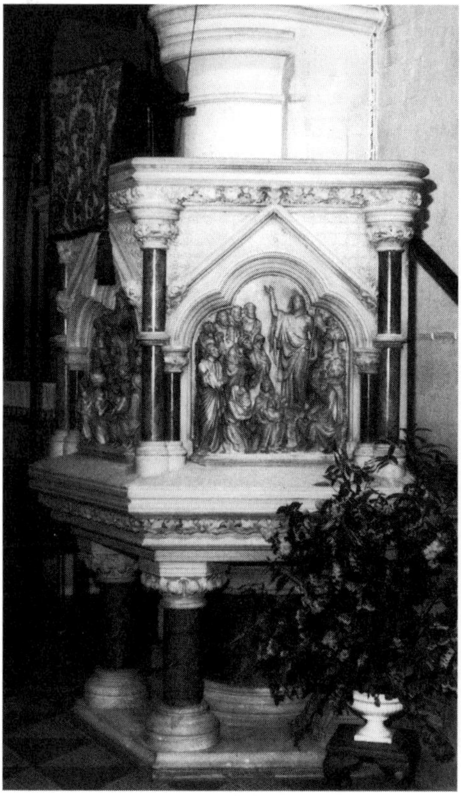

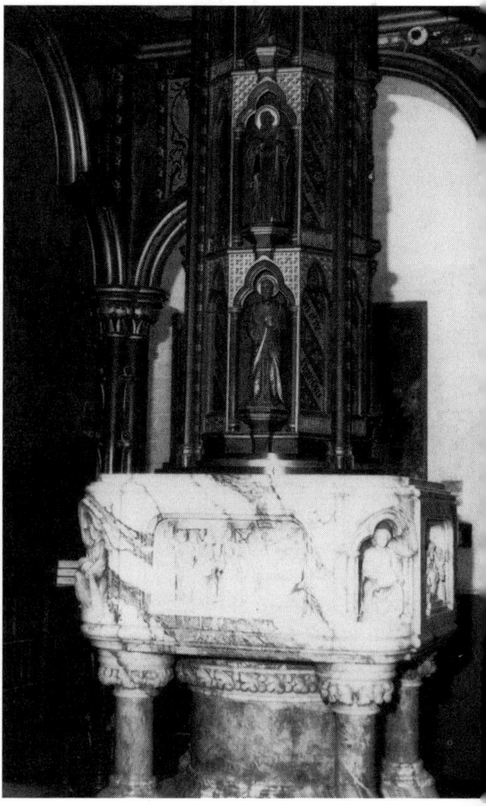

ABOVE: Duke of Albany Memorial, Christ Church, Esher. (OM) BELOW LEFT: St Nicholas' Church, Guildford: pulpit by Earp. (KMB) RIGHT: St Nicholas' Church, Guildford: font by Earp. (KMB)

Worthy of Note

In 1854 a new church called Christ Church was built in Esher, a large village on the Portsmouth Road in north-east Surrey, about fifteen miles from Central London. The architect was Benjamin Ferrey, a pupil of Pugin, and George Myers was the builder.

Queen Victoria had purchased Claremont, the mansion nearby, as a residence for her youngest son Leopold, Duke of Albany, upon his marriage. As is well known, the Duke died after only two years of married life.

The Queen ordered a monument for her son in the form of a bust by the Esher sculptor F.J. Williamson. It was first put in St George's Chapel, Windsor, but afterwards the Queen instructed it to be removed to Christ Church in Esher.

The bust was mounted in a monumental surround designed by William Blomfield and executed by Thomas Earp in alabaster, the whole making an impressive shrine for the late Duke overlooking the north aisle of Esher's church. On the opposite side is Williamson's memorial tablet to Helen, the Duchess of Albany, who survived her husband well into the 1920s.

In 1870 Thomas Earp was asked to undertake the provision of a memorial to a former distinguished rector of St Nicholas' Church, Guildford.

The rector was Thomas Goodwin Hatchard, who had been appointed to St Nicholas in 1856. He was the grandson of the founder of Hatchard's, the Piccadilly booksellers. On taking up residence in Guildford he brought with him his Jewish wife, whom he had met while on a mission to the Holy Land. She was a daughter of the then Bishop of Jerusalem, who was himself a convert from Judaism.

By the time of his appointment, however, St Nicholas was showing marked signs of deterioration. It was a very ancient church, believed to have been founded in the 11th century and had had many rebuildings. Little was done, however, until in 1870 a new rector, J.S.B. Monsell, appointed Teulon, Earp's great patron, to assess what should be done.

Meanwhile Thomas Hatchard had been appointed in 1867 to be Rural Dean of Stoke, and a year later was elevated to be Bishop of Mauritius.

He sailed to take up his appointment at once, but sadly his episcopate was short-lived. He died of a fever within a year after taking up duties in his new diocese.

His former parishioners at Guildford insisted that he should be suitably commemorated as part of the massive reconstruction that was taking place at St Nicholas'. Teulon had recommended a complete rebuilding as being relatively more economical than piecemeal repairs, but Teulon had died before the work got under way. The work was brought to its completion by Ewan Christian, the architect and adviser to the Ecclesiastical Commissioners.

Thomas Earp's memorial took the form of a pulpit to furnish the new church. The money for it was raised by special subscriptions. It followed conventional patterns, displaying carved reliefs of New Testament scenes. Earp also provided a font, which was paid for by an anonymous donor. For each of these works Earp was paid £150 which, in today's rate of currency, would be approximately £9,000.

The church of St Nicholas occupies a prominent position on the banks of the River Wey, near the foot of Guildford's steep main street. The green copper tower rooftop is a familiar feature of that townscape.

A different scene where work of Thomas Earp is to be found is in the drawing-room of Arundel Castle, which stands where the River Arun forms a gap through the South Downs of West Sussex.

Although Arundel Castle was founded in 1067 by William the Conqueror, one of a chain of strongholds set up along the South Coast as a precaution against reconquest by the seafaring Norse, the castle as it appears at present is really a product of 19th-century rebuilding and remodelling.

Successive Dukes of Norfolk, the landowners of the Castle and its grounds, initiated several schemes to develop a medieval fortress into a modern lavish residence fit for the entertainment of royalty.

The architect chosen for this undertaking was Charles Alban Buckler, the son of John Chessell Buckler, the antiquarian writer and church restorer. Previously some reconstruction had been undertaken by M.E. Hadfield, one of the architects for St Marie's, Sheffield, but these were not completed. The redevelopment proceeded on modern lines, electric lighting and *en suite* water closets being installed at the outset. This work was done during the 1870s.

The magnificent drawing-room featured a striking chimney-piece in Painswick stone executed by Thomas Earp, who is described by Dr J.M. Robinson, librarian to the Duke of Norfolk, as the 'doyen of Victorian architectural sculptors'.

This chimney-piece is adorned with a top cresting of strawberry leaves as on a ducal coronet, while capitals on either side possess strawberry leaves and Fitzalan oak leaves, relating to some of the ancestral forebears of the Howards, the family name of the present Dukes of Norfolk. For this work Thomas Earp was paid £150.

Alongside the castle and matching it in prominence is the church of Our Lady and St Philip Howard, which was built at the time of the redevelopments of the Castle by J.H. Hansom of Hansom cab fame. The builder was Thomas Earp's old master, George Myers.

This church is now a cathedral for the Catholic diocese of Arundel and Brighton.

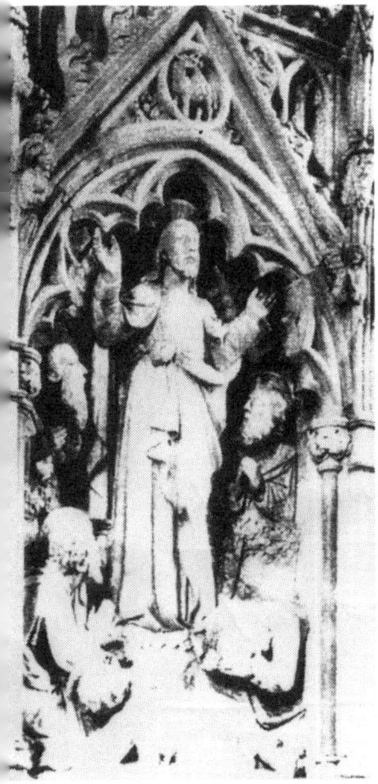

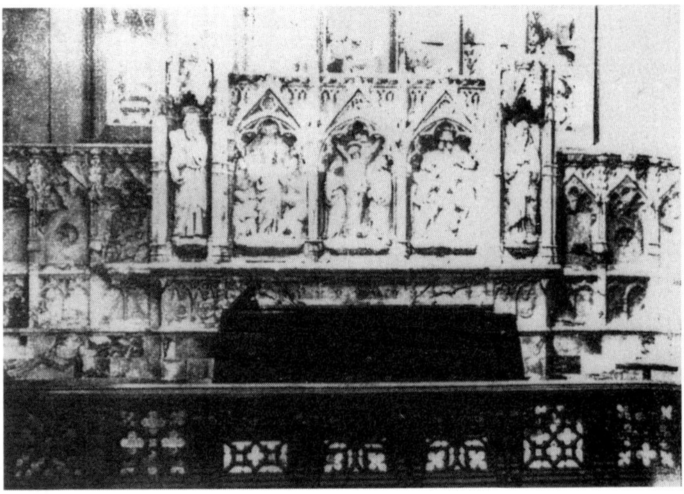

EFT: St Andrew's Cathedral, Sydney: replaced central panel of the reredos. (RAHS) RIGHT: St Andrew's Cathedral, Sydney: the reredos as at first installed. (RAHS)

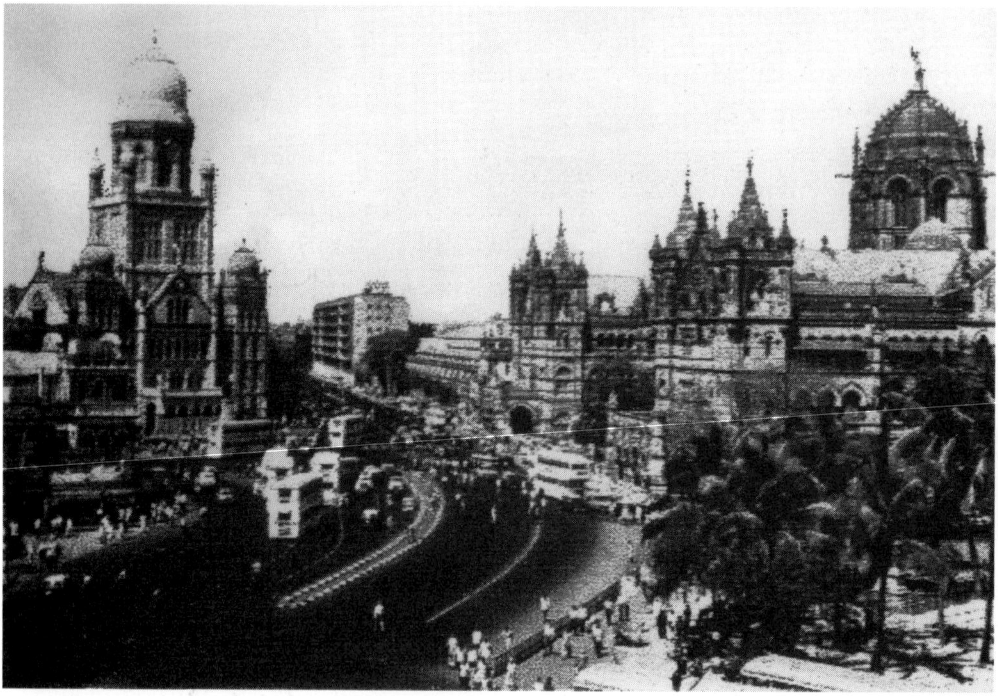

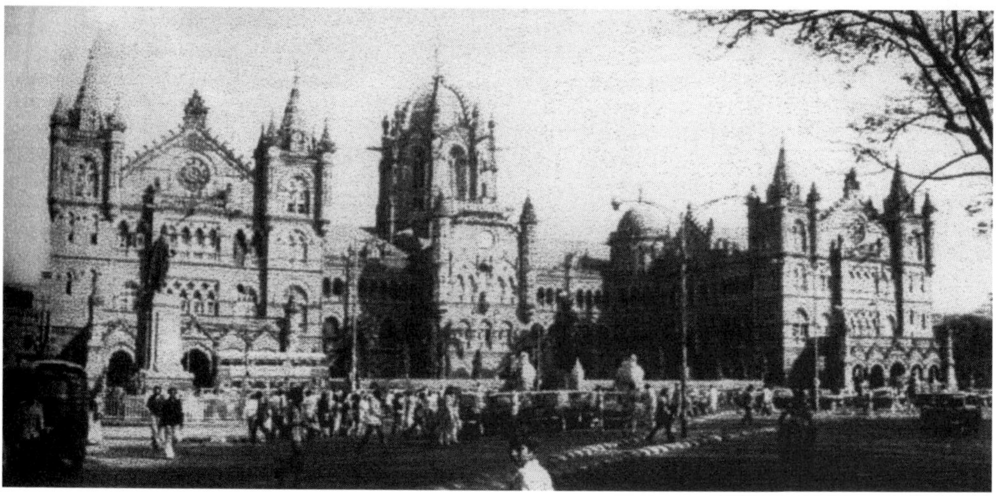

The Victoria Terminus, Bombay: Thomas Earp's 'Progress' statue in the top-right hand corner (ABOVE). (PM)

BEYOND THESE SHORES

In October 1886 a reredos designed and executed by Thomas Earp in London was despatched and delivered to St Andrew's Cathedral in Sydney, Australia.

St Andrew's Cathedral was begun in 1819 when the foundation stone was first laid by Governor MacQuarie, who had chosen as his architect one Francis Greenway. This work was never completed and the site was used for other purposes. A fresh start was made on another site in 1837 by Bishop Broughton, employing James Hume as architect. Again in 1842 work ceased due to lack of funds during a drought and consequent trade depression.

In 1846 Bishop Broughton made a fresh resolve to give Sydney its own cathedral and engaged a certain Edmund Blacket to bring the work to completion. Blacket was already a distinguished architect, having been responsible for many churches, schools, and public buildings throughout the colony (as it was then) and was not only the Diocesan Architect but had been appointed Colonial architect in 1849.

Under his guidance St Andrew's grew to be the stately and dignified building it now is, with Western towers matching in style and dignity those at Magdalen College, Oxford.

However, by the 1880s the original reredos at the High Altar had fallen into disrepair. The new Bishop, Dr Barry, commissioned J.L. Pearson to provide a new one. Pearson, who had already designed the Tudor Gothic library at Lincoln's Inn, London, and was about to be engaged on the building of Truro Cathedral, chose Thomas Earp to execute the new reredos.

The materials used were Caen stone, agate and alabaster. The reredos is divided into three panels by agate columns, and figures in alabaster are set against backgrounds of semi-transparent Caen stone. On each side stand figures of Moses and Elijah.

The three panels represented scenes from the life of Christ. They were, from left to right, the Resurrection, the Crucifixion, and the Ascension.

It was the second panel that aroused controversy as soon as it was installed. There was a strong evangelical element among the worshippers of St Andrews to whom a representation of the Cross and its Victim was distasteful and a sign of idolatry and superstition.

The Cathedral Chapter listened sympathetically to the objections of the protesters, of whose sincerity there could be no doubt. The matter was referred to the Diocesan Synod, who decided to commission an alternative design.

Thomas Earp therefore undertook to make a new panel to replace the 'Crucifixion' which was a portrayal of the 'Transfiguration', thereby making the flanking figures of Moses and Elijah more appropriate, for it was these persons who were seen to be accompanying Christ when He was transfigured in his glory in the sight of his disciples.

The cost of the alterations, including presumably the shipment of the replacing item, was handsomely met by the voluntary donations of the objectors. The eventual result stands as a particularly fine example of Christian sculpture.

Turning from a 'lowly shrine' for the King of Heaven to a soaring monument of triumph for an earthly sovereign, we may now discuss the great Chhatrapati Shivaji railway terminus in Bombay, which has, surmounting its central dome, a four-metre high statue representing 'Progress' made in the workshops of Thomas Earp.

Originally called the 'Victoria Terminus', this railway station building was completed in 1888, supposedly built over a shrine of the Koli goddess Mumba Devi. It was designed by Frederick William Stevens, who had held the office of architect to the Indian Government. He was a practitioner of Victorian Gothic architecture and was successful at mingling Gothic with Indo-Sarcenic styles.

The station building is modelled on the lines of St Pancras, London. Stevens brought about an unequalled fusion of marble, decorated tiles, stained glass, metal, concrete and bricks. The dome commands the centre of the complex, dwarfing the two wings of the building. Besides the statue of 'Progress', Thomas Earp carved the Imperial lion and the Indian tiger to flank either side of the main entrance gateway.

The station was opened to traffic in 1887, a little before its final completion, to celebrate the Golden Jubilee of Queen Victoria. The name was changed to its present one of Chhatrapati Shivaji, after the Maratha warrior, upon India becoming a republic, but it is still known as 'V.T.' Half a million commuters use it daily.

The Final Years

Then a shattering event jeopardised all Earp's plans for the continuity of the family business. Arthur died unexpectedly at Margate, and Arthur's widow, Emily, was left to bring up the eldest son, Walter, as well as two girls and two other boys.

This was the latest of many tragedies in the life of Thomas Earp. He had already lost two of Isabella's children in infancy. Another child from his second marriage died before she was one. His hopes now centred on Edgar, his only son by Ellen, as someone to whom he could hand on the business, and his grandson Walter, still an infant.

The work of the firm went on. Thomas would arrive daily at his workshops, examining designs, selecting stones. allocating tasks to his workmen or travelling to sites where building work was in progress, often to remote parts of the country, using the steam railway, or by coach to places where the railway had not yet come. On arrival he would supervise the work and ensure the correct position of artefacts. Much of this was performed in Caen stone, easy to work, not too costly, and for that reason acceptable to many clients.

He had a reputation for being conscientious and thorough. In appearance he was somewhat thick-set and stocky, with a round face and pointed, stubbly beard. His eyes were keen and penetrating, and his jaw was firm, with a slight thrust to his underlip. He had a somewhat sharp temper. He abhorred seeing people with their hands in their pockets, adjudging them 'idle men'. In politics he had an antipathy to Gladstone (who, it was believed, dozed during sermons from the pulpit carved by Earp at St Swithins, Bournemouth), but was a keen supporter of Disraeli. Two of Earp's employees, McCarthy and Knox, became assistants to John Francis Bentley during the later building of Westminster Cathedral.

For his relaxation he may have attended the Canterbury Theatre, or any of the others south of the Thames. Licensing restrictions had for many years forbidden the extensive opening of theatres in the West End or City, apart from Drury Lane or Covent Garden Opera House: no such restriction operated on the other side of the river.

For personal and other reasons the 1880s were not easy for Thomas.

The Gothic Revival and the widespread building of churches and other public buildings had passed their peak. In 1887 Queen Victoria celebrated her Golden Jubilee. Most of the great buildings and town halls of the Kingdom were completed or nearing completion. The needs of worshippers in Britain's towns and cities were met. Nevertheless, much business still came the way of Earp and Hobbs.

Street's posthumous designs for the rebuilding of the Guard's Chapel, Birdcage Walk, Westminster, were completed at the turn of the decade, and Earp's font, together with Street's chancel, today remain the sole surviving relics of the Victorian structure destroyed by a German flying bomb in 1944. The font stands beneath the lofty roof of the rebuilt modern chapel, a poignant memorial to the obscenity of war, that killed over 200 people while at worship.

In St Margaret's Convent, East Grinstead, Sussex, there is a splended altar-piece executed by Earp and his partner, Hobbs between 1879 and 1883. St James's Church, Croydon, possesses a reredos made by him in 1884.

Thomas Earp's important contribution to the restoration work at Rochester Cathedral, where Pearson was carrying on restorations started by Scott earlier that century, was the new font.

The font was formerly in the centre of the nave by the west door, but has since been moved to its present position in the south aisle. It is a pleasing example of Earp's work in polished granite, conspicuous in its situation beneath one of the sweeping Norman arches of the nave. Of all the cathedrals that I have visited, searching for Earp's work, I find Rochester the most homely and intimate.

At St Neots, Huntingdonshire, F.W. Walters designed a monument for the tomb of the Rowley family in the Church of St Mary the Virgin. The Rowleys were a local family of note, and church benefactors. Mrs Rowley had died in 1886, and Thomas Earp's recumbent effigy of her can still be seen behind a closely-wrought grille on the north side of the chancel.

About the time this memorial was prepared and installed, Thomas's second wife, Ellen, died.

She was buried in Nunhead Cemetery, London, in a grave, the burial rights of which he had already bought, and which he also intended to occupy. Upon a simple sandstone cross he carved the inscription: 'Eternal Rest grant to her, O Lord, and let perpetual light shine upon her'.

For Thomas Earp, the days that followed the death of Ellen would have been days for taking stock, reviewing his work and achievements since he first came to London in 1850.

There had been many vast changes in the architectural world: Scott, Barry, Pugin and Street had all made way for newcomers Pearson, Sedding, Shaw and Bentley. Thomas Earp and his partnership no longer worked exclusively for one architect. His work enhanced the devotional atmosphere of worshippers of many persuasions — Anglicans, Catholics, Irvingites, Presbyterians, Episcopalians. There had been, for the whole of his career, much competition for contracts from such firms as Farmer and Brindley, situated close by in the Westminster Bridge Road, and sculptors such as Redfern and Edward Wyon.

His daughters from his first marriage were relatively settled, as securely as could be expected in a world full of hazards: Isabella Caroline had married David Jenkins in 1870 and Edith Florence married John Painter in 1880. His younger family may well have presented him with a problem, for he had appointed his son Arthur guardian of his younger children. Ethel, his eldest daughter by Ellen, in 1889 married Robert Thomas, a butcher of Lower Marsh, Lambeth.

There was little time left to Thomas to see more of his family set up home. The *Building News* of 15 September 1893, carried an obituary notice that speaks for itself:

'We regret to learn, just as we go to press, that cholera has found a victim in Mr. Earp, the well-known sculptor, of Kennington-road, Kennington, S.E. Mr. Earp was first seized with pains on Saturday, but took no heed of them. On Tuesday evening, however, he became so seriously ill that he was removed to St. Thomas's Hospital, where in spite of all care, his death supervened on Wednesday morning. On the morning of the day he was removed to the hospital, Mr. Earp was out, busy, directing the operations of his workmen.'

He died on 12 September 1893. He was buried in the grave in Nunhead Cemetery where Ellen had lain for five years.

Today the grave is almost concealed by undergrowth and the wording all but obliterated. The man whose lifetime was spent providing so many monuments for others has a barely recognisable tombstone for himself.

So lived and died Thomas Earp, sculptor and stone and wood carver of Lambeth. His work had given substance and permanence to the ideas of the Barries, the Scotts, Street, Butterfield, Blomfield, Teulon and many others who had helped to make the Victorian scene what it was. His lifetime coincided with those of William Morris, John Ruskin, Dante Gabriel Rossetti, Holman Hunt, Madox-Brown, Burne-Jones, and Lord Leighton. His work is to be found in villages, towns and cities throughout the United Kingdom, and this book has described only a fraction of them.

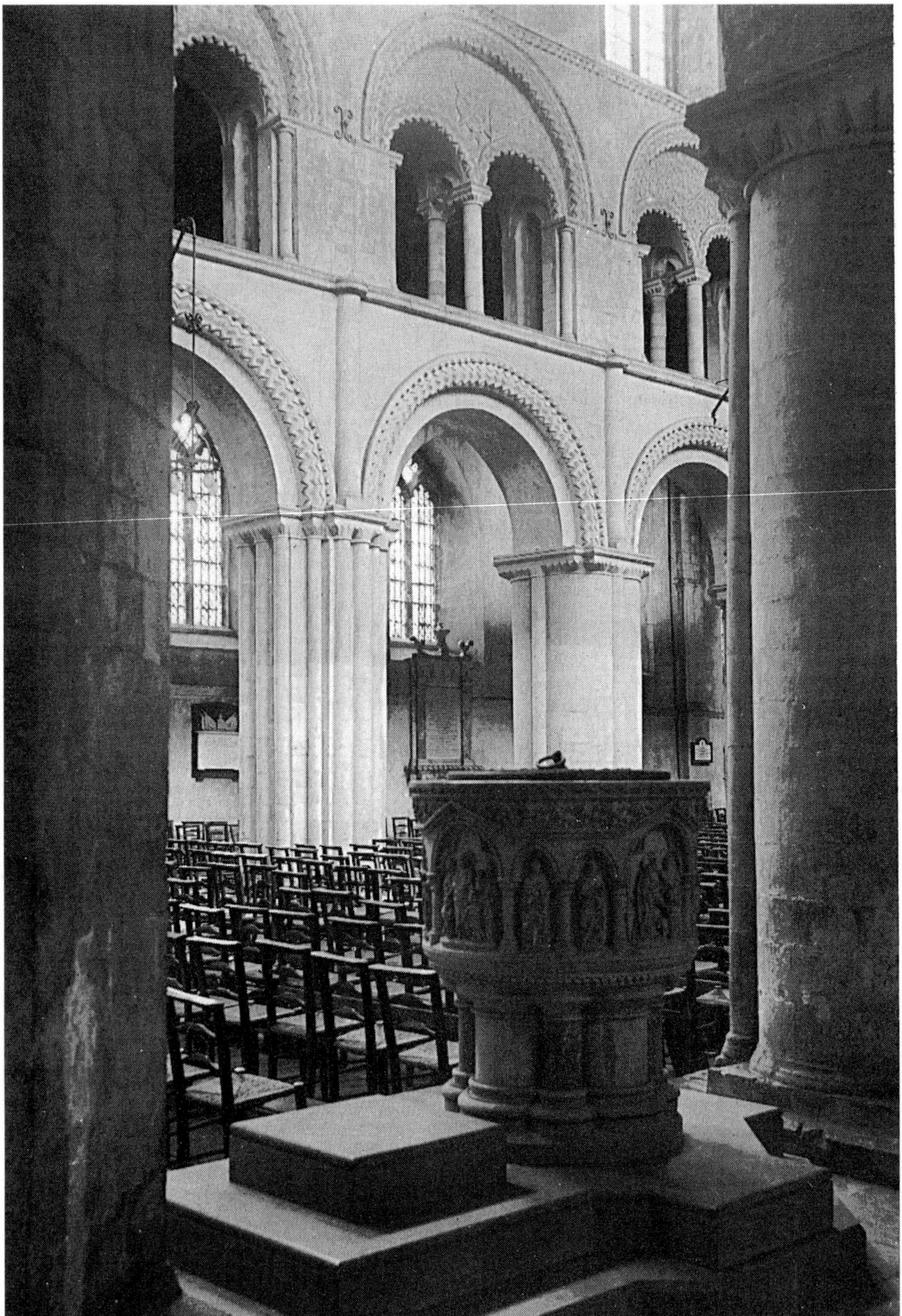

Rochester Cathedral: nave and font. (NMR)

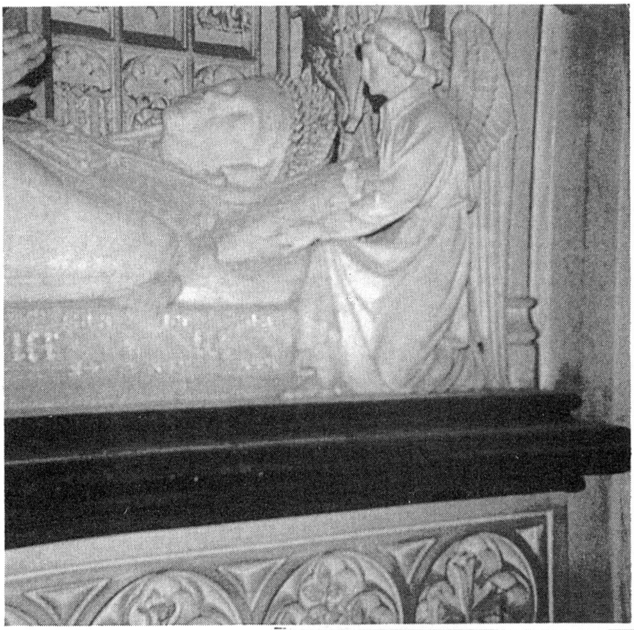

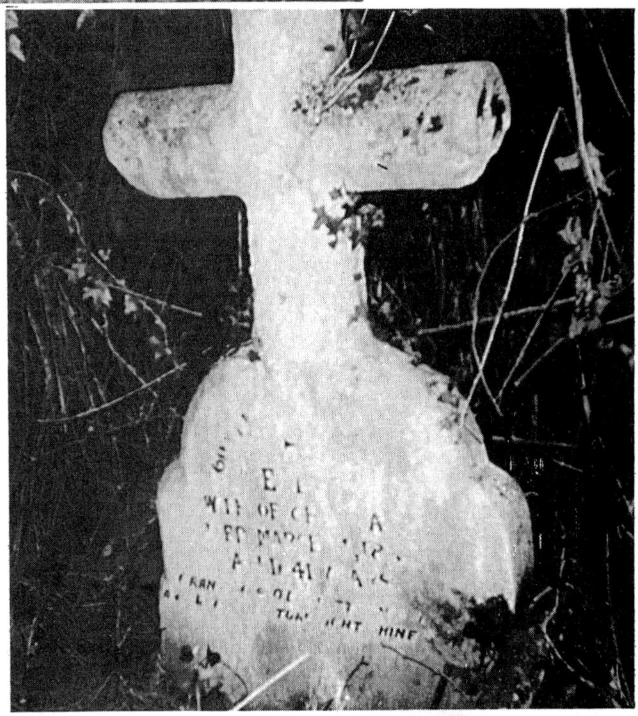

ABOVE: Church of St Mary the Virgin, St Neots: detail of the Rowley Monument. BELOW: Thomas and Ellen Earp's gravestone in Nunhead Cemetery.

Appendix 1

For many years after Thomas Earp's death Earp and Hobbs carried on business. An advertisement in the *Ecclesiastical Art Exhibition Catalogue* held at Rhyl in 1892 reads:

'THOMAS EARP & E. HOBBS,
Architectural Sculptors in Marble, Alabaster, Stone and Wood.
Sculptors of the Reredos, St. Thomas's Church, Rhyl.

LONDON: 49 Kennington Road, Lambeth, S.E.
MANCHESTER: 63 Lower Mosley Street.

Reredoses, Fonts, Pulpits, Monuments, &c
Executed in any Material and Fixed in any part of the Country: also the Carving of Churches and Public Buildings, by an Experienced Staff of Carvers.'

The partnership traded until 1974, when it was taken over by J. Whitehead and Son, of Kennington Oval, London.

APPENDIX 2

EARP'S OTHER WORK
A list of other locations of Earp work not mentioned in the book. This list is not exhaustive.

Abberley, Worcestershire. St Mary's, c1876. Carved capitals
Ashby de la Zouch, Leicestershire. St Helens, c1880. Alabaster pulpit and font
Backwell, Somerset. St Andrews, 1873. Reredos
Berrieuw, Powys. St Bueno 1896. Reredos
Broadstairs, Kent. St Peter's. 1868. Reredos
Croydon, St James's. 1884. Reredos
East Coatham, Oxon. Grammar School chapel c1870. Reredos
Edinburgh, Grange. St Margaret's Convent Lady chapel 1877. Reredos
Great Fawley, Berks. St Mary's 1866. Reredos
High Wycombe, Bucks. All Saints 1875. Font
Leeds. St Peter's, Kirkgate. Reredos 1872.
Llandysilio, N. Wales. St Tysilio 1868. Reredos
London: Clapton. All Saints (demolished) Reredos
Holborn. No 87 Chancery Lane. Exterior carvings 1864
Paddington. Holy Trinity, Bishops Bridge 1864 (demolished) Reredos (with E. Hobbs)
Montgomery, Powys. St Nicholas, Trefoldwyn. 1878. Reredos
Peasemore, Berks. St Barnabas 1866. Reredos
Pewsey, Wilts. St John the Baptist c1861. Pulpit, lectern & stalls
Sheppingley, Hunts. St Lawrence's 1859-60. All wood-and stone-carving.
Uppingham, Leics. School chapel 1874. Pulpit.
Welshpool, Powys, St Mary's 1870. Reredos
Wootton Bassett, St Bartholomew & All Saints. Reredos.

Bibliography

Printed Works

Campbell, Daniel. *St Peter's Church, Bournemouth*

Chambers, J.D. *Modern Nottingham in the Making* (1945)

Church, R.A. *Economic & Social Change in a Midland Town — Victorian Nottingham 1815-1900*

Clarke, Basil F.L. *Church Builders of the 19th century* (1938) SPCK — do — *Parish Churches of London* (1966)

De L'Hopital, W. *Westminster Cathedral and its Architect* (1919)

Eastlake, Charles. *History of the Gothic Revival* (1872)

Fawcett, Jane (ed). *Seven Victorian Architects* (1976) Thames & Hudson

Gleicher, Lord Edward. *London Open-air Statuary*

Greater London Council. *Survey of London* (sundry volumes)

Hadfield, Charles. *History of St Marie's Mission & church*

Howell, Peter (ed). Letters from Bentley to Hadfield (from *Architectural History* Vol 23, 1980)

Jarvis, Simon. *High Victorian Design*

Jones, E. & Woodward, C. *The Architecture of London*

Kidson, Peter, Murray, Peter & Thompson, Paul. *A History of English Architecture* (1965) Pelican Books

McQueen, Ian. *Bournemouth St. Peter's* (1971) Dorset Publishing Co

Mitchell, Anthony. *Esher, A Pictorial History* (1995)

Muthesius, S. *The High Victorian Movement in Architecture* 1850-1870 (1972)

Pevsner, N. *The Buildings of England* (sundry volumes)

Read, Benedict. *Victorian Sculpture* (1982) Yale University Press

Robinson, John Martin. *Arundel Castle* (1994)

Saint, Andrew. *Richard Norman Shaw* (1976) New Haven & London

Scott, G.C. *Personal and Professional Recollections*

Spencer-Silver, Patricia. *Pugin's Builder* (1993)

Stamp, Gavin & Amery, Colin. *Victorian Buildings of London 1837-1887* (1980)

Street, A.E. *Memoir of G.E. Street* (1888 reprinted 1972)

Taylor, Brian. *The Lower Church* (Guildford, 1980)

Thompson, Paul. *William Butterfield* (1971)

Van Loo, Gerald. *A Victorian Parson* (1989)

Newspapers and Periodicals

The Architect

The Builder

The Building News

Other Sources
Deardon's Nottingham Directory 1834
Ecclesiologist, The
Exhibition Catalogue, 1851
Exhibition Catalogue, 1862
London Post Office Directories 1851-1879
Mumbai (Indian Tourist Agency)
National Biography, Dictionary of
Nottingham Council Meetings — *Minutes*
Phillimore's *Marriage Registers — Derbyshire and Nottinghamshire*
Pictorial History of Chester Cathedral (guide book)
Royal Australian History Society (*Journal & Proceedings* 1946)
St Philip & St James (Oxford) church guide book
St Paul's Ecclesiological Society *Transactions* (Vol I)
The Architect, August 1877
The Building News, January 1868
White's Nottingham Directory 1844

KEY TO CAPTION CREDITS

(BN)	*Building News*
(DCN-S)	David C. Neil-Smith
(EHNMR)	English Heritage (NMR)
(GH)	Reverend G. Hurst
(GLC)	Greater London Council
(KMB)	Kenneth M. Bryant
(KR)	Keith Reedman
(OM)	Olive Mitchell
(N)	His Grace the Duke of Norfolk
(NMR)	National Monuments Record
(NMRW)	National Monuments Record for Wales
(PL/FUC)	Pauline Lord & Friends of Union Chapel Islington
(PM)	Paul Mitchell
(PS)	Paul & Sue Spice
(RAHS)	Royal Australian Historical Society
(RIBA)	Royal Institute of British Architects

Index

Figures in *italics* refer to illustrations

Note to original index:

for 99, read 117; 100, read 118; 101, read 119; 102, read 120 and for 103, read 122

INDEX ADDENDA

Italics refer to illustrations